Essays & Studies 1986

The English Association

The object of the English Association is to promote understanding and appreciation of the English language and its literature.

The Association is an international organization with branches at home and overseas. Its activities include sponsoring a number of publications and organizing annual sixth-form conferences.

Publications

The Year's Work in English Studies. An annual bibliographical survey of scholarly books and articles on English, American and Commonwealth Literature and Language. Published by John Murray (USA: Humanities Press).

Essays and Studies. An annual anthology of essays usually on a wide range of subjects from the medieval to the modern. A collector is nominated every year by the Association. Published by John Murray (USA: Humanities Press).

English. The journal of the Association, *English* is published three times a year by the Oxford University Press.

The Presidential Address. The Presidential Address, usually on a literary or linguistic subject, is published annually.

News-Letter. A *News-Letter* is issued three times a year giving information about forthcoming publications, conferences, and other activities.

Occasional Publications. The Association has published or sponsored many occasional works including *A Guide to Degree Courses in English* (Sixth Edition 1982), *English Grammar For Today*, *English Short Stories of Today*, *Poems of Today*, and many pamphlets.

Membership

There are three categories of membership. Full members receive copies of *The Year's Work in English Studies*, *Essays and Studies*, *English* (3 issues), three *News-Letters* and the Presidential Address.

Ordinary Members receive *English* (3 issues), three *News-Letters* and the Presidential Address.

Member Schools receive two copies of each issue of *English*, one copy of *Essays and Studies* (optional), three *News-Letters* and the Presidential Address. Schools Membership also offers preferential booking for Sixth Form Conference places.

For further details write to The Secretary, The English Association, 1 Priory Gardens, London W4 1TT.

Essays & Studies
1986

Collected by
G. A. Wilkes

JOHN MURRAY, LONDON
HUMANITIES PRESS, ATLANTIC HIGHLANDS, N.J.

ESSAYS AND STUDIES 1986
IS VOLUME THIRTY-NINE IN THE NEW SERIES
OF ESSAYS AND STUDIES COLLECTED ON BEHALF OF
THE ENGLISH ASSOCIATION

© The English Association 1986

First published 1986
by John Murray (Publishers) Ltd
50 Albemarle Street, London W1X 4BD

Typeset by Fakenham Photosetting Ltd, Fakenham, Norfolk
Printed and bound in Great Britain at
The Bath Press, Avon

British Library Cataloguing in Publication Data

Essays and studies.—Vol. 39—1986
1. English literature—History and criticism—
Periodicals
820.9   PR1

ISBN 0-7195-4282-0

Humanities Press ISBN 0-391-03404-9

Contents

Dante's 'Astripetam Aquilam' and the Theme of Poetic Discretion in the 'House of Fame'[1]

JAMES SIMPSON

Recent criticism of the *House of Fame* has elucidated in particular a scepticism in the poem towards any claims to certainty and absoluteness which might be made for received tradition,[2] and it is this scepticism which motivates and justifies Geffrey's interest in the quotidian and unstable world represented by his final destination, the House of Rumour. For however quotidian in concern that destination might be—quite unlike, say, the resplendent and authoritative destination to which the dreamer in *Pearl* aspires— Geffrey's willingness to be taken to the Domus Dedaly is nevertheless intelligible and intelligent given the consistent unreliability of authoritative sources in the poem. Examples of this unreliability are manifold, but by way of encapsulating the poem's treatment of such sources, one could point to the lament of Dido against 'wikke Fame' in Book I: this lament not only reminds us of Virgil's description of *Fama* in Book IV of the *Aeneid*, '*tam ficti prauique tenax quam nuntia veri*'[3] (which is the source glossed marginally by both the Fairfax and the Bodley manuscripts), but it also alerts us to the fact that Virgil's own, supposedly authoritative account of the Dido/Aeneas relationship may itself be called into question, may itself be an example of 'fals and soth compouned'

[1] I should like to thank Dr A.S.G. Edwards for his helpful comments on an earlier draft of this essay.

[2] See in particular S. Delany, *Chaucer's 'House of Fame': The Poetics of Sceptical Fideism* (Chicago and London, 1972); the recent article by J.T. Miller, 'The Writing on the Wall: Authority and Authorship in Chaucer's *House of Fame*', *Ch. Rev.*, 17 (1982), 95–116, and J.M. Fyler, *Chaucer and Ovid* (New Haven and London, 1979), ch. 2.

[3] *Virgil*, with a translation by H. Rushton Fairclough (London and Cambridge, Mass., 1957), *Aeneid*, IV.188 (the edition from which translations will be drawn). Chaucer was also familiar with the topos through Boccaccio's *Filostrato*, Bk. IV, stanza 78: '*La fama velocissima, la quale / il falso e 'l vero ugualmente rapporta*' (ed. V. Branca, in *Tutte le Opere di Giovanni Boccaccio*, 6 vols. (Verona, 1964), Vol. II), which Chaucer translates in *Troilus and Criseyde*, IV.660.

(11.1029 and 2108).[4] The authoritative source is evoked, that is, precisely in order that it be questioned.

That authoritative sources are questioned in this way is, one could add, more generally suggested both by the unsettling experience of reading Book I, in which the criticism of Aeneas as a 'traytour' sits uneasily beside the attempt to excuse him 'ful-lyche of al his grete trespas' (1.427), and by the arrangement of the poets in Book III, where the contradictions of the first book are underlined in a more abstract way by the collocation of Vergil, bearing up 'the fame of Pius Aeneas' (1.1485), with Ovid, 'Venus clerk', from whose *Heroides* derives the tradition more sympathetic to Dido.

But if Geffrey's choice of mundane matter in the Domus Dedaly derives from the recognition that authoritative texts and voices may be questioned, I should like to argue here that this questioning is concomitant with a respect for, and a deference towards, the capacities of great poets which are beyond those of Geffrey (or Chaucer) himself. This is suggested by an interesting parallel from Dante's *De Vulgari Eloquentia* especially, but also by comparison with a passage in Horace's *De Arte Poetica*, at points where both Dante and Horace are concerned with the discretion a poet must exercise in choosing his matter. That discretion in such a choice is an important theme in the *House of Fame*, is also suggested by a range of loci in the poem which are illuminated by the parallels with Dante and Horace.

I

In his article, 'Chaucer's Eagle: A Contemplative Symbol',[5] J.M. Steadman clearly presents the evidence from both patristic and poetic tradition to argue that the eagle in the *House of Fame* is a 'contemplative symbol', representative of the kind of dream-guide who offers revelation of divine and stable truth. It is certainly true that the eagle's first appearance in the poem suggests precisely this tradition: the narrator prays to Christ to be delivered from 'fantome' and 'illusion', in response to which the eagle descends. The words 'fantome' and 'illusion' here are drawn from a set of technical words used to describe dreams, and designate nightmarish dreams of no

[4] All quotations from the *House of Fame*, and other works by Chaucer, are from *The Works of Geoffrey Chaucer*, ed. F.N. Robinson, 2nd edn (Oxford, 1957).
[5] *PMLA*, 75 (1960), pp. 153–9.

predictive significance.[6] And if they do suggest one kind of vision which is in no way contemplative, the sight of the eagle does promise, by contrast, divine revelation:

> But this as sooth as deth, certeyn,
> Hyt was of gold, and shon so bryghte
> That never sawe men such a syghte,
> But yf the heven had ywonne
> Al newe of gold another sonne.   (11.502–6)

These lines are drawn from a web of Dantean associations related to the eagle, and to the supra-human power of understanding represented by that bird. In *Paradiso* I.48 Dante remarks that '*aquila sí non li s'affisse unquanco*', when he sees Beatrice look directly into the sun; he then looks into the sun himself since, he says, much is granted there which is beyond human powers on earth. He is unable to look for long, but long enough to have the experience of an apparently miraculous increase of light:

> *E di subito parve giorno a giorno*
> *essere aggiunto, come quei che puote*
> *avesse il ciel d'un altro sole adorno.*   (I.61–3)

And if this context suggests a divine vision, so too does the further Dantean source of especial importance here, the eagle of *Purgatorio* IX.20, '*con penne d'oro*', which appears as Dante dreams in early dawn, when the mind '*alle sue vision quasi è divina*' (IX.18).[7]

The sources of the lines, then, do point us towards the tradition of

---

[6] For the technical context of these words, see W.C. Curry, *Chaucer and the Medieval Sciences* (London, 1960), pp. 209–14; for discussion of dream terminology in the poem, see also F.X. Newman, 'House of Fame 7–12', *ELN*, 6 (1968), pp. 5–12, and E. Giaccherini, 'Una *Crux* Chauceriana: I Sogni nella *House of Fame*', *Rivista di Letteratura Moderne e Comparate*, 27 (1974), pp. 165–76. For the wider meaning of 'fantoume' see S. Delany, *Chaucer's 'House of Fame'*, pp. 58–68.

[7] The edition from which I am citing these passages is *La Divina Commedia*, ed. N. Sapegno, 3 vols. (Florence, 1979). For the Dantean source of these lines, see Skeat's note to 1.500 in *The Works of Chaucer*, 6 vols. (Oxford, 1894), III.253, and D.A. Dilts, 'Observations on Dante and the *House of Fame*', *MLN*, 57 (1942), pp. 26–8. For a more sceptical view of Dante's influence here, and a review of all the relevant scholarship, see H.H. Schless, *Chaucer and Dante: a Revaluation* (Norman, Oklahoma, 1984), pp. 46–9.

contemplative visionary experience which Steadman outlines. And the Proem to Book II insists, indeed, that the vision offered by the eagle was of this kind. In contrast to the breathless and bemused presentation of dream theory in the Proem to Book I, here the narrator states in a definitive way that his dream was quite certainly of elevated significance, offering the opposite of dreams which could be designated by the words 'fantome' and 'illusion'; here he declares to the reader that he will relate

> So sely an avisyon,
> That Isaye, ne Scipion,
> Ne kyng Nabugodonosor,
> Pharoo, Turnus, ne Elcanor,
> Ne mette such a drem as this! (11.513–17)

The word 'avisyon' designates dreams of high philosophic and predictive significance,[8] of the kind experienced by the biblical and classical figures to whom the narrator here refers, in which the soul, 'of propre kynde'

> Be so parfit, as men fynde,
> That yt forwot that ys to come,
> And that hyt warneth alle and some
> Of euerych of her aventures
> Be avisions, or be figures. (11.43–7)

But if Steadman is right in setting the eagle within a tradition of contemplative, visionary writing, the very certainty of the declaration in the Proem to Book II, quite unlike anything else in Chaucer's dream poetry, and quite inconsistent with the quality of the dream itself, might give us pause to consider how Chaucer is manipulating this tradition within the *House of Fame*; he seems to me to be provoking expectations of visionary matter, in order to underline his deliberate, discreet choice of different, more unstable subjects for his poetry. At this point the parallel from the *De Vulgari Eloquentia* is, I think, helpful.

In Book II.4 of *De Vulgari Eloquentia*, Dante offers a different,

[8] s.v. *MED* 1(a). The evidence for translating 'avisioun' at 1.7 as 'a false or meaningless dream' (s.v. *MED* 1(b)) is uncertain, particularly when the word quite certainly designates a dream of high philosophic significance at 11.48 and 513. It will be clear that I agree with Newman, '*House of Fame* 7–12', against Giaccherini, 'Una *Crux* Chauceriana', with regard to the meaning of 'avisioun'.

though related context in which an eagle appears, which may be relevant to consideration of the eagle in the *House of Fame*. Dante defines the judgement required by a poet in choosing matter which he is capable of handling; this is the first decision the poet must make:

> *Ante omnia ergo dicimus unumquemque debere materie pondus propriis humeris coequare, ne forte humerorum nimio gravata virtute in cenum cespitare necesse sit: hoc est quod Magister noster Oratius precipit cum in principio Poetrie 'Sumite materiam' dicit.*

> [First of all, therefore, we say that any writer must balance the weight of his poetic matter to his own shoulders, lest by charging them with too great a weight he should tumble into the mud; this is what our master Horace teaches when, at the beginning of his *Art of Poetry*, he says 'Select a matter . . .']

He ends the chapter by warning those who are incapable of sustaining the tragic style against attempting to do so in this way:

> *Sed cautionem atque discretionem hanc accipere, sicut decet, hoc opus et labor est, quoniam numquam sine strenuitate ingenii et artis assiduitate scientiarumque habitu fieri potest . . . Et ideo confutetur illorum stultitia qui, arte scientiaque immunes, de solo ingenio confidentes, ad summa summe canenda proprumpunt; et a tanta presumptuositate desistant; et si anseres natura vel desidia sunt, nolint astripetam aquilam imitari.*

> [But to exercise caution and this discretion, as is fitting, this is the real task, since it cannot be achieved without profound effort of mind, constant practice in the art, and acquired knowledge . . . So let the stupidity of those be confounded who, without art and knowledge, trusting solely in their own wit, rush forward to sing of the highest things in the highest style; let them desist from such presumption, and if they are geese by nature or by idleness, then let them not wish to imitate the star-seeking eagle.][9]

---

[9] Edited by P.V. Mengaldo, *Vulgares Eloquentes*, 3 (Padua, 1968), p. 39. I have emended the reading *'unumquenque'* in Mengaldo's text to *'unumquemque'*, and I have also adopted the reading of mss. G and T for *'hoc opus'*, where Mengaldo adopts the reading of B, *'hic opus'*. For the translation, I have partly relied on that of S. Purcell (Manchester, 1981). The only other suggestion in Chaucer criticism that Chaucer may have drawn from the *De Vulgari Eloquentia* is in the article by D.K. Fry, 'The Ending of the *House of Fame*', in *Chaucer at Albany*, ed. R.H. Robbins (New York, 1975), pp. 27–40 (p. 32), as listed in L. King Morris, *Chaucer Source and Analogue Criticism, a Cross-Referenced Guide* (New York, 1985). This article offers no more concrete evidence than I am able to that Chaucer was familiar with this work of Dante.

The '*astripetam aquilam*' of this passage, as I understand it, is also drawn from the tradition to which Steadman draws attention; with the clause '*hic opus et labor est*', Dante recalls a passage from *Aeneid* VI, in which the Cumean Sibyl describes the daunting prospect before Aeneas as he descends to the underworld, from which only the blessed few have been able to escape to rise thereafter to the heavens:

> *sed revocare gradum superasque evadere ad auras,*
> *hoc opus, hic labor est. pauci, quos aequus amavit*
> *Iuppiter aut ardens evexit ad aethera virtus,*
> *dis geniti potuere.*   (VI. 129–31)

[. . . but to recall thy steps and pass out to the upper air, this is the task, this is the toil! Some few, whom kindly Jupiter has loved, or shining worth uplifted to the heaven, sons of the gods, have availed.]

But Dante places this Virgilian expression of divine favour in a specifically poetic context, to suggest the capacities of those poets who are capable of sustaining matter of an elevated, visionary kind.[10]

The connection between Dante's '*astripetam aquilam*' and the *House of Fame* is curiously close: before Geffrey arrives at the House of Fame itself, which is 'betwixen hevene, erthe, and se' (1.715), he is offered a journey of a different kind by the eagle, to the heavenly regions of the stars. After Geffrey wonders whether he is in heaven 'in body or in gost', we read the following dialogue:

> 'Lat be', quod he, 'thy fantasye!
> Wilt thou lere of sterres aught?'
> 'Nay, certeynly', quod y, 'ryght naught'.
> 'And why?' 'For y am now to old'.

[10] One could add here, too, that Dante's understanding of the *De Arte Poetica* at this point is consonant with the scholia on Horace's work. Conrad of Hirsau (d. circa 1150), for example, in his *Dialogus super Auctores*, says this about Horace's intention:

> *Intendit autem in hoc opere poetarum aliquorum supercilium reprehendere, qui nomen quidem scriptorum usurpantes opus indiscreto stilo cuderunt nec modum vel ordinem debitum operi suo dedicarunt.*

The text is available in *Accessus ad Auctores*, ed. R.B.C. Huygens (Leiden, 1970), p. 113.

> 'Elles I wolde the have told',
> Quod he, 'the sterres names, lo,
> And al the hevenes sygnes therto,
> And which they ben'.   (11.992–9)

Unlike Dante's solicitous and attentive Vergil, with whom the eagle is implicitly paralleled,[11] the eagle is a strangely rash dream-guide, apparently unaware of the limitations of his pupil. The fact that he is impulsive here, in contrast with the tradition which would describe him as the representative of contemplative vision, is consistent with the parodic treatment of the eagle as a dream-guide throughout the poem. But what the parallel with *De Vulgari Eloquentia* points us to in particular is the rashness of the eagle in the context of a discussion about proper *poetic* discretion. The eagle had described his mission to Geffrey as being an offer, by way of reward, of new poetic matter; he explains that Jove wishes to reward Geffrey because he has

> . . . no tydynges
> Of Loves folk yf they be glade,
> Ne of noght elles that God made.   (11.644–6)

However vague the expansive gesture of the last line cited here is, the eagle's relation of Jove's command puts the emphasis firmly upon the unstable, sublunary world of

> . . . loves casuelly
> That ben betyd, no man wot why,
> But as a blynd man stert an hare.   (11.679–81)[12]

From 1.992, though, when the eagle proposes to offer Geffrey matter of a much more elevated kind, through a journey to the stars, it is Geffrey himself who insists upon his own limitations, and, in contrast to the conventional relations between a dreamer and his guide, it is Geffrey who instructs his guide in matters of self-knowledge which cannot, ultimately, be taught—the 'caution and discretion' a poet should exercise in choosing his matter.

---

[11] For this parallelism, see the references assembled by P. Toynbee, *Dante in English Literature* (London, 1909), pp. 6–7.

[12] For the important theme of Geffrey's search for new matter in the poem, see R.C. Goffin, 'Quiting by Tidings in the *House of Fame*' *MAE*, 12 (1943), pp. 40–4.

This self-awareness is stated, too, in terms which suggest not merely personal limitations, but specifically poetic limitations. Geffrey persuasively resists the impulsive desire of the eagle to fly to the stars both by stating his personal limitations, and by stressing his preparedness to trust those poets who have written about the heavens:

> 'No fors', quod y, 'hyt is no nede.
> I leve as wel, so God me spede,
> Hem that write of this matere,
> As though I knew her places here;
> And eke they shynen here so bryghte,
> Hyt shulde shenden al my syghte,
> To loke on hem'.   (11.1011–16)

By saying that he will trust those who have written of the heavens, Geffrey thereby defers to those poets whose capacities were such as to sustain description of this kind—specifically, one might assume, Martianus Capella and Alain de Lille, who are referred to in 11.985/6. Such a literary deference is also implicit in the ostensibly personal remark that his sight will be unable to bear the brightness of the stars. The implication here that the writers who have described the heavens could sustain that light is corroborated by reference to texts which are closely behind Chaucer's poem: in Alain de Lille's *Anticlaudianus*, Phronesis is unable to sustain the light of the Empyrean until she is aided by Faith, who gives her a mirror, by which 'her eyes recover, find a kindly brightness and enjoy the clear, gleaming light';[13] and in the *Paradiso*, too, Dante's capacity and desire to comprehend the mysteries of God is conceived of in terms of his ability to see, in what would normally be a blinding glare; in the passage drawn from the first canto to which I referred earlier, for example, Dante follows Beatrice in fixing '*li occhi al sole oltre nostr' uso*', or in the twenty-third canto, Beatrice aids Dante to sustain the overwhelming light of Christ shining forth from among the

[13] Translated by J.J. Sheridan (Toronto, 1973), p. 160. For Chaucer's debt to Alain de Lille more generally, see P. Dronke, 'Chaucer and the Medieval Latin Poets', in *Geoffrey Chaucer*, Writers and their Background, ed. D. Brewer (London, 1974), pp. 154–72.

triumphant redeemed, to mention but two of many relevant examples from *Paradiso* especially.[14]

So Geffrey, in accordance with the kind of warning made by Dante in the *De Vulgari Eloquentia*, refuses to follow the '*astripetam aquilam*', and this refusal is felt in precisely the terms the passage from Dante offers us—those of *poetic* discretion. That Chaucer was familiar with the *De Vulgari Eloquentia* is unlikely: the work was not at all widely known, with only three surviving manuscripts from the fourteenth century (all from the second half of the century), two of which were probably copied in Padua (MSS G and T), while the third was also copied in Northern Italy.[15] All we can say is that Chaucer passed through northern Italy in his first Italian journey of 1372/3 (possibly through Padua), and stayed in Lombardy for about six weeks in 1378.[16] Certainly the author of a work so profoundly influenced by the *Divine Comedy* as is the *House of Fame* would have been eager to read any other work by Dante, and especially a work of Dante which, despite its many local concerns, had bearing upon Chaucer's own poetic enterprise in the vernacular.

II

The passage from *De Vulgari Eloquentia* remains of interest, however, not simply for the phrase '*astripetam aquilam*', but more generally, and more importantly, for the way in which the context of that phrase illuminates the theme of poetic discretion in the poem as a whole. I shall now turn to discussion of this theme as it is manifest elsewhere in the poem, without attempting to posit the *De Vulgari Eloquentia* passage as a source: it is useful insofar as it helps to

---

[14] Other relevant loci in the *Paradiso* are V.1; XIV.76; XIII.85; XXIII.118; XXV.118; XXVI.1; XXX.118; XXXIII.25; XXXIII.52, and XXXIII.82. Given the discussion of Phaëthon below, it may also be relevant to notice that Ovid describes Phaëthon's inability to sustain the light of heaven at the moment he realizes he has flown too high:

> . . . *palluit et subito genua intremuere timore*
> *Suntque oculis tenebrae per tantum lumen orbortae.*

(*Metamorphoses*, ed. F.J. Miller (London and New York, 1916), II.180–1)

[15] Mengaldo, pp. xvii–xix.

[16] *Chaucer Life Records*, ed. M.M. Crow and C.C. Olson (Oxford, 1966), pp. 32 and 53. For the possibility that Chaucer travelled through Padua on his return journey, see G.B. Parks, 'The Route of Chaucer's First Journey to Italy', *ELH*, 16 (1949), pp. 174–87 (p. 185).

illuminate the *House of Fame*; the precise relation between the two texts must remain a matter for conjecture.

The narrator's willingness to trust those poets who have written about the heavens in Book II is matched by his deference towards those who have described the lower world in Book I. His account of Aeneas's voyages after leaving Dido is cursory, and makes a special point of referring the reader to those poets who have described the underworld:

> And every turment eke in helle
> Saugh he, which is longe to telle;
> Which whoso willeth for to knowe,
> He moste rede many a rowe
> On Virgile or on Claudian,
> Or Daunte, that hit telle kan. (11.445–50)

And if Geffrey is unwilling to attempt a description of the underworld in Book I, and a journey to the heavens in the second book, this may, I think, be understood by the exempla preceding Geffrey's refusal of the eagle's offer to soar to the stars; for these exempla do stress the folly of exceeding one's proper limitations. The eagle asks Geffrey at 1.991 if he can recognize any place on earth; in response to Geffrey's timid 'Nay', the eagle asserts that this is not surprising, since Geffrey is higher than other figures who have had authoritative visions: Alexander, and Scipio,

> That saw in drem, at poynt devys,
> Helle and erthe and paradys. (11.917–18)

These figures (whose range of experience in fact exceeds that of Geffrey) are placed beside those of Dedalus and Icarus, where the emphasis falls, in however cursory a way, upon the failure of Icarus,

> That fleigh so highe that the hete
> Hys wynges malt, and he fel wete
> In myd the see, and ther he dreynte. (11.920–22)

But if this is a passing reflection upon one who, through a failure to know his own limitations, attempted to fly too high into the heavens, it is followed by another exemplum which is moralized in such a way as to focus more explicitly on the dangers of self-ignorance. After mentioning Icarus, the eagle encourages Geffrey to turn his gaze even higher, and to consider the Galaxy. Here he offers, in an apparently gratuitous way, the exemplum of Phaëthon, who was unable to control his chariot at such dangerous heights. The eagle not only briefly recounts the narrative of Phaëthon's disastrous journey, but also appends a short moralization:

> Loo, ys it not a gret myschaunce
> To lete a fool han governaunce
> Of thing that he can not demeyne?   (11.957–9)

However offhand the eagle's moralization here might seem, comparison with other moralizations of Ovid reveals that the emphasis is carefully chosen. In the *Ovide Moralisé*, for example, the legend of Phaëthon is interpreted in different ways: he is euhemeristically described as having been an ignorant astonomer (II.645–88), or allegorized as the Pope guiding the doctrine of the Church (II.731–913), or as Antichrist (II.914–1012). Chaucer, however, who seems certain to have been familiar with this work, chooses to emphasize the following, purely moral interpretation offered by the French poem:

> *Par le cas Pheton puet entendre,*
> *Qui bien i veult exámple prendre,*
> *Que nulz ne se doit orgueillir*
> *De trop grant emprise acueillir,*
> *Mes chacuns se maint a mesure,*
> *Lonc son pooir et sa nature.*
> *Trop est folz qui d'orgeuil se charge,*
> *Et qui sor soi prent si grant charge*
> *Qu'il n'en puet la paine endurer.*
> *L'oms orgueilleus ne puet durer*
> *Longement quil ne li meschiee.*[17]

And in the *Ovidius Moralizatus* by Petrus Berchorius, the legend of Icarus is treated in the same way. Like Phoebus, who warns

---

[17] Edited by C. de Boer, Verhandelingen der Koninklijke Akademie Van Wetenschappen (Amsterdam, 1915–38), II.688–97. For Chaucer's knowledge of the French text, see J.L. Lowes, 'Chaucer and the *Ovide Moralisé*', *PMLA*, 33 (1918), pp. 302–25; S.B. Meech, 'Chaucer and the *Ovide Moralisé*—a Further Study', *PMLA*, 45 (1931), pp. 182–204; S. Delany, 'Chaucer's *House of Fame* and the *Ovide Moralisé*', *Comparative Literature*, 20 (1968), pp. 254–64; and A. Minnis, 'A Note on Chaucer and the *Ovide Moralisé*', *MAE*, 48 (1979), pp. 254–7.

Phaëthon to take '*la moienne voie*' in the French text (VIII.1636), Dedalus is reported as instructing his son that

> ... *nec huc nec illuc ad stellas respiceret: sed recte, mature, medie, continue post se iret.*

[... that he should not look hither and thither towards the stars, but that he should go behind him directly, at the proper time, moderately, and continuously.][18]

And after the fall of Icarus, the event is moralized in this way:

> *Dicitur exemplariter contra filios inobedientes et presumptuosos qui patrem suum vel prelatum vel sapientes viros sequi nolunt vel eorum mandatis obedire: immo seipsos fatue praeponunt et ardua opera ultra vires facere vel attemptare praesumunt quae ad finem deducere non possunt.*

[This is said, by way of example, against disobedient and presumptuous children who are not willing to follow either their father, or their master, or wise men, just as they are unwilling to obey their directions; on the contrary, they stupidly put themselves in charge, and presume to do or to attempt difficult enterprises beyond their powers, which they are unable to bring to an end. (p. 128)]

J.A. Dane has argued in a recent article that this apparently gratuitous legend and its moralization can be applied to the eagle himself; given the eagle's readiness to fly ever higher, which is emphasized immediately after his moralization of the Phaëthon legend ('And with this word, soth for to seyne,/ He gan alway upper to sore ...'—1.960), Dane points out that the eagle 'completely ignores its [the moralization's] relevance to his own actions', and that 'he is no better judge of the moral force of the legend of Phaëthon than he is of the moral force of another Ovidian legend he cites a few lines earlier [that of Icarus]'.[19]

This argument is persuasive, but it should, I think, be extended to focus on the corresponding discretion of Geffrey in not being so

---

[18] The text is Bk. XV of Berchorius' *Reductorium Morale*, ed. J. Engels, Werkmaterial, iii (Utrecht, 1966), p. 128. The translation is mine.

[19] 'Chaucer's Eagle's Ovid's Phaëthon: A Study in Literary Reception', *JMRS*, 2 (1981), pp. 71–82 (p. 80).

presumptuous as to take on poetic matter beyond his own powers. It is true that Geffrey is 'gladded' by the eagle's high soaring (1.962), but his recollection of 'Boece' at this point causes him to 'wexen in a were'. He quotes Boethius by referring to the capacity of thought to pass beyond the mundane:

> . . . A thought may flee so hye,
> Wyth fetheres of Philosophye,
> To passen euerych element;
> And whan he hath so fer ywent,
> Than may be seen, behynde hys bak,
> Cloude.   (11.973–8)

But if Boethius's *'pennae'* are invoked here as a 'symbol of contemplation' (as J.M. Steadman has argued), the context of the reference would suggest not that Chaucer is emphasizing 'the purely intellectual character of his journey',[20] but rather that such a symbol is invoked precisely in order to underline the fact that Geffrey will *not* take on contemplative matter for his poetry, and that he will not journey to the stars. The passage cited from Boethius here reads thus in Chaucer's own *Boece*:

> I have, forthi, swifte fetheris that surmounten the heighte of hevene. Whanne the swifte thoght hath clothid itself in tho fetheris, it despiseth the hateful erthes, and surmounteth the rowndnesse of the gret ayr; and it seth the cloudes byhynde his bak, and passeth the heighte of the regioun of the fir, that eschaufeth by the swifte moevynge of the firmament, til that he areyseth hym into the houses that beren the sterres, and joyneth his weies with the sonne, Phebus. (IV.ml)

Geffrey does reach the point at which he sees the 'cloudes behynde his bak', but this the moment at which he declines the eagle's invitation to fly to the 'houses that beren the sterres', and, in so doing, as I argued earlier, he curbs the rashness of the eagle by stating his own limitations. Like his contemporary Gower, who chooses the 'middel weie',[21] and who declares about himself that it is not in 'my sufficance' to 'strecche up to the hevene/ Min hand' (I.1–2), Chaucer

---

[20] Steadman, 'Chaucer's Eagle', p. 159.
[21] *Confessio Amantis*, ed. G.C. MacCaulay, in *The Complete Works of John Gower*, 7 vols. (Oxford, 1899), prologue, 1.17.

prefers not to fly to the region of the stars, but instead to visit the
House of Fame, which is

> Ryght even in myddes of the weye
> Betwixen hevene, erthe, and see.   (11.714–15)[22]

III

If Geffrey's refusal, then, to follow the '*astripetam aquilam*' may, as
I have argued, be conceived of in the terms Dante offers us in the *De
Vulgari Eloquentia*—those of the '*discretio*' and '*cautio*' which a poet
must exercise in choosing his matter, then the same can be said for
his intelligent rejection of the House of Fame itself as a place in which
he might receive matter appropriate to his own interests and
capacities as a poet. I alluded earlier to the fact that the criticism of
authority implied in the unsettling juxtaposition of the Ovidian and
Virgilian traditions in Book I was underlined in a more abstract way
in the third book by the collocation of Virgil

> That bore hath up a longe while
> The fame of Pius Eneas,   (11.1484–5)

with Ovid, 'Venus clerk'. Juxtapositions of this kind would imply
that, however much Geffrey is prepared to believe the writings of
those poets who are able to take on matter concerned with the fixed
and stable afterworlds of heaven or hell, he is also willing to criticize
authoritative poets when their matter is earthly in concern, and
within Chaucer's own range of interest and capacity.

The manner by which this criticism is made is, however,
characteristically discreet—it is made 'silently, almost
imperceptibly, as if without knowing it, certainly without
ostentation', as J.A.W. Bennett has put it.[23] The very fact that these
poets are bearing their matter on 'shuldres hye' (11.1435, 1462,
1500), itself would imply respect for them. Like Dante, who asks his

---

[22] This would seem to be a translation of Ovid's lines describing the place
of the House of *Fama*:

> *Orbe locus medio est inter terrasque fretumque*
> *Caelestesque plagas, triplicis confinia mundi . . .*
>   (*Metamorphoses*, XII.39)

[23] J.A.W. Bennett, *Chaucer's 'Book of Fame'* (Oxford, 1968), p. 144.

reader to take into account '*il ponderoso tema / e l'omero mortal che se ne carca*' (*Paradiso* XXIII.64) (at a point when he feels unable to describe the quality of his experience), Chaucer here evokes the Horatian prescription referred to in the *De Vulgari Eloquentia*, that poets should take matter upon their shoulders which they are capable of sustaining:

> *Sumite materiam vestris, qui scribitis, aequam*
> *Viribus et versate diu quid ferre recusent,*
> *Quid valeant umeri.*

[You who write, select a matter equal to your powers, and consider for a long time what your shoulders refuse to bear, and what they are able to sustain.][24]

Chaucer's homage to the great poets in the House of Fame is evident here, however, given that they are capable of sustaining their considerable subjects; unlike Dante's depiction of his shoulder trembling under the weight of his '*ponderoso tema*' in the passage to which I have just referred, Chaucer's representation of these authoritative poets not only evokes, but also fulfils Horace's prescription.

Neither does Chaucer wish to contend with these great poets; unlike the poets challenging Homer's account of the matter of Troy, who have towards Homer 'a litil envye' (1.1476), or the foolhardy Marcia on the House of Fame, who

> . . . loste her skyn,
> Bothe in face, body, and chyn,
> For that she wolde envien, loo!
> To pipen bet than Apolloo,   (11.1229–32)[25]

Geffrey affirms his own conception of himself as a poet in terms which are not competitive, but which are, rather, founded upon an

---

[24] *De Arte Poetica* in Horace, *Epitres*, ed. F. Villeneuve (Paris, 1967), 11.38–40. The translation is mine. For the way in which Horace was received in the Middle Ages, see A. Monteverdi, 'Orazio nel medioevo', *Studi Medievali*, 9 (1936), pp. 162–180.

[25] For Chaucer's source for the figure Marcia, see A. David, 'How Marcia Lost her Skin: A Note on Chaucer's Mythology', in *The Learned and the Lewed, Studies in Chaucer and Medieval Literature*, Harvard English Studies, 5, ed. L.D. Benson (1974), pp. 19–31.

assured knowledge of both personal and artistic limitations. The reference to Marcia here may remind us of the invocations to both the *Paradiso* and the *Purgatorio*, in both of which reference is made to the poetically presumptuous. In Canto I of the *Paradiso*, for example, Dante sets his own uniquely ambitious poetic enterprise in the context of the presumptuous Marsia, who foolishly challenged Apollo to a musical competition (I.19–22). *Purgatorio*, too, begins with a reference to a mythological musical contest, in which the Pierides challenged, and were defeated by, the Muses (I.10–12). It is this contest which, amusingly, is recalled by the Man of Law in the Introduction to his tale, when he compares his own poetic skill with that of Chaucer:

> But of my tale how shal I doon this day?
> Me were looth be likned, doutelees,
> To Muses that men clepe Pierides—
> *Methamorphosios* woot what I mene;
> But nathelees, I recche noght a beene
> Though I come after hym with hawebake.
> I speke in prose, and lat him rymes make.   (11.90–6)

But however much Chaucer is claiming, through the Man of Law, poetic superiority for himself here (and however light and amusing his claim), the stance of Geffrey in the *House of Fame* is better characterized by reference to the epilogue of *Troilus and Criseyde*, where the narrator bids farewell to his 'litel ... tragedye', and instructs it not to 'envien' any other poetry,

> But subgit be to alle poesye;
> And kis the steppes, where as thow seest pace
> Virgile, Ovide, Omer, Lucan, and Stace.   (V.1790–2)[26]

  But the fact that he will not 'envie' other poetry does not mean that Geffrey will not distinguish himself from the authoritative traditions

---

[26] It will be clear that I understand 'envien' at both *Troilus and Criseyde* V.1789 and *House of Fame* 1.1231, to mean 'to contend or to vie with another in rivalry' (*MED*), since both examples of the word are found in contexts concerning (poetic) rivalry. In this I agree with *MED* against *A Chaucer Glossary*, compiled by N. Davis et al. (Oxford, 1979), where the example from *Troilus and Criseyde* is listed under the other meaning of 'envien', 'to feel ill-will towards, to resent'.

represented by the poets in the House of Fame, and this act of critical separation is felt, I think, in precisely the terms of poetic discretion I have been concerned to illuminate in this essay. After witnessing the humiliating subjection to chance which Fame's petitioners must undergo, Geffrey is asked at 1.1871 to give his name, and to say whether or not he has come to have fame. However much, as J. A. W. Bennett has pointed out, the *House of Fame* is 'the first English narrative poem . . . in which the author . . . names himself' (p. 164, n.1), when asked for a specific declaration of his identity, Geffrey declines; it is his answer to the second question (whether or not he has come to have fame), which clarifies his failure to answer the first:

> 'Nay, for sothe, frend', quod y;
> 'I cam noght hyder, graunt mercy,
> For no such cause, by my hed!
> Sufficeth me, as I were ded,
> That no wight have my name in honde.
> I wot myself best how y stonde;
> For what I drye, or what I thynke,
> I wil myselven al hyt drynke,
> Certeyn, for the more part,
> As fer forth as I kan myn art'.   (11.1873–82)[27]

There is an implied, though quiet criticism of the great poets in Fame's house here, insofar as the reputations their authority has established are associated with the arbitrary 'casuel' action of Fame herself. Geffrey desires, as he goes on to say, 'tydynges' for his poetry, and his modest, unpretentious definition of the kind of matter he wishes to hear suggests the mundane and unstable matter of everyday experience, which has not yet been fixed by the decree of Fame:

> Somme newe thinges, y not what,
> Tydynges, other this or that,
> Of love, or suche thynges glade.   (11.1887–9)

But if there is any criticism here of that poetry which has been fixed by Fame, it is almost completely displaced by the quality of Geffrey's

[27] For the seriousness with which Dante names himself, see *Convivio*, ed. M. Simonelli, Testi e Saggi di Letterature Moderne, II (Bologna, 1966), I.ii.3, and *Purgatorio*, XXX.53–63. For the question more generally, see E. R. Curtius, *European Literature and the Latin Middle Ages*, translated by W. R. Trask (London, 1953), pp. 515–17.

own statement of his personal and poetic position in 11.1873–82, whose humble, colloquial style does not belie the centrality of its meaning: Geffrey's self-knowledge is felt to rest not upon Fame, but rather, 'for the more part', upon his understanding of his art. The matter of that art will not be the elevated matter of the great poets in the House of Fame, but, rather, the unstable, various, and absorbing matter of everyday experience. But however much Geffrey does accept unstable matter of this kind, before which he will be observant and unassuming, we can nevertheless sense in this statement the stable note of the poem; this stability is to be found not in the quality of the poem's matter, but rather in the voice of Geffrey himself, whose affirmation here that personal responsibility will be dependent on artistic self-knowledge is consonant with his discreet refusal to follow the presumptuous 'astripetam aquilam'.

'Mouldy Tales': The Context of Shakespeare's 'Cymbeline'

DAVID L. FROST

I presume that most of the English-speaking world has heard Alan Bennett's sermon from *Beyond the Fringe*:

> Life, you know, is rather like opening a tin of sardines—we're all of us looking for the key . . . Others think they've found it, don't they? They roll back the lid of the sardine-tin of life, they reveal the sardines, the riches of life therein, and they get them out, they enjoy them—but, you know, there's always a little bit in the corner you can't get out. I wonder, is there a little bit in the corner of your life? I know there is in mine.

Almost as well known is the story told me by Canon Cyril Taylor from the Salisbury and Wells Theological College of a group of ordinands receiving instruction in the art of the sermon, who were sat down to hear an edited tape of Bennett's satire—and found nothing to laugh at.

Their problem was one of defining context: nothing in their situation indicated anything other than the devotional, so they misread Bennett's signals. Knowledge of context is particularly necessary to the detection of humour, irony, satire, parody and burlesque; yet in the case of our older literature much of the necessary context has perished beyond the hope of reconstruction. Professor R. A. Foakes set Marston critics a pretty problem in 1962,[1] when he suggested that *Antonio and Mellida* and *Antonio's Revenge* were sophisticated send-ups by child actors of the huffing and puffing of their elders on the public stage. The problem has yet to be resolved, for in a poetic tradition already so conceited and bombastic it is hard to be sure where the high style tips over into recognizable excess—Jonson for one seems to have taken Marston at face value. And there is the difficulty of distinguishing what is deliberately

---

[1] R. A. Foakes, 'John Marston's Fantastical Plays: *Antonio and Mellida* and *Antonio's Revenge*', *Philological Quarterly*, 41 (1962), pp. 229–39.

excessive from what is merely incompetent: one recalls
Shaftesbury's complaint against late seventeenth-century
panegyrists, who were so inept that they had inadvertently invented
the encomiastic satire. My present purpose is to suggest—and our
limited knowledge allows us only to suggest—that we have sat
through Shakespeare's *Cymbeline* with altogether too reverential an
expectation: we have seen its context as Shakespeare, and therefore
as high-minded and serious art, whereas the milieu of *Cymbeline*,
insofar as we can reconstruct it, suggests a work which may be as
near to the spirit of the sermon in *Beyond the Fringe* as it is to *The
Tempest* or to *The Winter's Tale*.

Though by the late 1600s Romance might seem to be the
dominant fictional form, not only in general esteem but in its variety
of modes, in the number of translations from foreign sources, and in
sheer bulk of writing, its supremacy had not gone unchallenged. If in
verse Spenser's *Faerie Queene* and in prose Sidney's *Arcadia* were for
their serious moralizing and instructional purpose among the most
admired works of the age, protests had been raised against the
salacious Romances of writers like Chettle, who pandered to the
emergent taste for what C.S. Lewis once called 'literary fare "for
tired businessmen" '.[2] Probably more influential than complaints
from moralists were the strictures of critics such as Sidney,[3]
Puttenham,[4] and Jonson against Romance plays that violated neo-
classical canons of unity, and only a handful of stage Romances seem
to have been performed in London from 1600 till the appearance of
Pericles in late 1607 or thereabouts.[5]

Cervantes's satire on chivalric Romance was known to Francis
Beaumont by 1608, some while before the publication of the first
English translation of *Don Quixote* by Thomas Shelton in 1612.
Though Beaumont's *Knight of the Burning Pestle*, probably
performed in 1607 or 1608, failed to please the very mixed audience
who patronized the Children of the Revels, his burlesque was not
entirely inopportune, given the developing influence of Jonson in

[2] C.S. Lewis, *English Literature in the Sixteenth Century Excluding Drama*
(Oxford, 1954), p. 310.

[3] Sir Philip Sidney, *Works*, ed. A. Feuillerat, 4 vols. (Cambridge, 1912–
26), III.38.

[4] G. Puttenham, *The Arte of English Poesie*, ed. G.D. Willcock and A.
Walker (Cambridge, 1936), p. 83.

[5] See A. Harbage (ed.) and S. Schoenbaum (reviser), *Annals of English
Drama, 975–1700* (Philadelphia, 1964).

literary and in Court circles as a critic and as a writer of plays and masques. The outstanding success of *Pericles* seems particularly to have provoked that 'Empyrick'[6] poet to attack stage Romances that 'runne away from Nature'[7] as much as they violate neo-classic principles: perhaps Jonson was insensitive to the symbolic dimension Shakespeare had given to the form, for his 'Ode to Himself' written in 1629 recalled only how audiences had flocked to 'some mouldy tale / Like Pericles', neglecting his own more serious efforts.[8] In the Induction to *Bartholomew Fair* (1614) he declared himself 'loth to make Nature afraid in his *Playes*, like those that beget *Tales*, *Tempests*, and such like *Drolleries*',[9] and to Drummond of Hawthornden in 1618 he commented on the Romance absurdity of a sea-coast in Bohemia.[10]

One further circumstance surrounding the appearance of *Cymbeline* is the strange case of *Mucedorus*, of which the Third Quarto was published in 1610 (according to its title-page)

Amplified with new additions, as it was acted before the Kings Maiestie at White-hall on Shroue-sunday night. By his Highnes Seruants usually playing at the Globe.

Mucedorus was a primitive stage Romance of the 1580s, first published in 1598 and popular with unsophisticated audiences— apprentice Rafe in *The Knight of the Burning Pestle* had starred as 'Mucedorus before the wardens of our company'.[11] The play was revived in the City of London at least once in the early part of James's reign, for the Quarto of 1606 substitutes references to James for those to Elizabeth.[12] But after performance by the King's Men

---

[6] A 'meere Empyrick, one that getts what he hath by observation, and makes onely nature privy to what he endites', an abusive contemporary reference to Jonson in *2 The Return from Parnassus*, I.i.294–9, ed. J.B. Leishman, *The Three Parnassus Plays* (London, 1949), p. 244.

[7] *The Alchemist*, 'To the Reader', l.7, *Ben Jonson's Works*, ed. C.H. Herford, P. and E. Simpson, 11 vols. (Oxford, 1925–52), V.291.

[8] Ode appended to *The New Inn*, *Ben Jonson's Works*, ed. Herford and Simpson, VI.492.

[9] ll.129–30, *Ben Jonson's Works*, ed. Herford and Simpson, VI.16.

[10] 'Ben Jonson's Conversations with William Drummond of Hawthornden', *Ben Jonson's Works*, ed. Herford and Simpson, I.128.

[11] Induction, l. 83, *The Knight of the Burning Pestle*, ed. Michael Hattaway, New Mermaid (London, 1969).

[12] See Richard T. Thornberry, 'A Seventeenth-Century Revival of *Mucedorus* in London before 1610', *Shakespeare Quarterly*, 28 (1977), pp. 362–4.

around 1610 *Mucedorus* ran through another fifteen editions, becoming the most frequently printed play of the period.

The 1610 Prologue and Epilogue addressed to the King make it most unlikely that the claim of a Court revival is untrue, but there has been some unwillingness to accept the ascription to the King's Men, chiefly because *Mucedorus* is such lame stuff, but also because the Epilogue apologizes for an offensive play presented in the actors' theatre, and we know of no such offence given by the King's Men at that time. What has not been sufficiently noticed is the terms in which Comedy in the Epilogue brushes off Envy's threats to raise a poet whose 'high abuse' will bring the players into danger or restraint of playing:

> Ha, ha, ha! I laugh to heare thy folly;
> This is a trap for Boyes, not Men, nor such,
> Especially desertfull in their doinges,
> Whose stay'd discretion rules their purposes.
> I and my faction doe eschew those vices.[13]

I suggest that the play apologized for is one presented by the Children of the Blackfriars, who were threatened by James with a permanent ban after their performance in 1608 of Chapman's *Byron* and who were again in difficulties that year over a lost play by Marston which presented the King as drunk and bad-tempered, made unflattering references to James's silver mines in Scotland, and subsequently landed the author in Newgate Prison.[14] The Blackfriars Theatre was owned by Burbage, the leading actor of the King's Men, and two months after Marston's imprisonment a King's Men syndicate took over the lease of the theatre. It may well be that Burbage felt some responsibility for plays presented in his theatre (especially since the French Ambassador reports James as threatening all theatres with closure), and appended to his next Court performance an apologetic disclaimer that rejects the 'trap for Boyes, not Men', talks of an 'vnwilling errour', and insists on the 'stay'd discretion' of *his* 'faction', who 'eschew those vices'. According to the 1610 Quarto, *Mucedorus* can be performed by as

[13] Epilogue, ll. 54–8, *The Comedie of Mucedorus*, ed. C.F. Tucker Brooke, in *The Shakespeare Apocrypha* (Oxford, 1908), pp. 125–6.
[14] E.K. Chambers's argument in *The Elizabethan Stage*, 4 vols. (Oxford, 1923), II.53–4, that Marston was author of the offending play has commanded wide assent.

few as ten actors, and it may be that the play was presented at Court by a remnant of the King's Men in 1608, 1609, or in early 1610, when the full company had been dispersed as a consequence of restraints on public playing in time of plague.

But why present *Mucedorus*? Partly, I think, because so old-fashioned a play was clearly innocent of meaning, let alone of factious intent; but chiefly, I would suggest, because the King's Men decided to make amends by the common method of clowning, of making fools of themselves before an offended superior. They deliberately hammed up an old play. This is not to say that James's Court would not have enjoyed a simple Romance tale; but it is hard to see how an audience who had seen the same actors in *Hamlet*, *Macbeth*, *Lear*, or *Othello* could have failed to mix with their enjoyment of the narrative of *Mucedorus* a sophisticated mirth at its naïveties. It must have been rather like watching Olivier do *Little Red Riding Hood* after a successful run in the tragedies of Ibsen. And there is the strong possibility that Shakespeare's *Cymbeline*, which probably followed the Court staging of *Mucedorus* and was almost certainly written before July 1610,[15] was evoked by and influenced by the unexpected success of *Mucedorus*'s revival.

The external evidence that might help us to give Shakespeare's *Cymbeline* its proper context is scant and ambiguous; we must therefore look to the play itself for hints as to how it is to be received—and here the evidence is necessarily cumulative. It is surely axiomatic that drama of any distinction dictates the mode of its playing: an actor who attempts to guy a speech from *Hamlet* makes only himself ridiculous. But the texture and language of *Cymbeline* seem to dictate a mode of playing that is peculiar. Harley Granville-Barker saw in its verse 'a new Euphuism' of imagination: expression 'will often be simple enough; it is the thought or emotion behind that may be too far-fetched for the occasion or the speaker'.[16] This pervasive inappropriateness of what is said to the character or to the situation of the sayer demands from an actor a less than full emotional

[15] The public theatres were closed by plague from August 1608 to December 1609. In July 1610 Arabella Stuart and William Seymour were imprisoned because of their secret marriage, and it would have been most unwise for Shakespeare to have written a play about the marriage of a princess to a commoner after this event.

[16] H. Granville-Barker, *Prefaces to Shakespeare* (1930; one volume edition, London: Batsford, 1972), I, p. 498.

involvement in his role, and encourages him to concentrate on merely local effects. The point can be made economically by reference to an early seventeenth-century setting of Cloten's aubade to Imogen that survives in the Bodleian Library and was possibly composed by Robert Johnson for an early performance of the play.[17] The suitor has been advised to provide dawn music to promote his oafish and adulterous advances: 'Come on, tune: if you can penetrate her with your fingering, so: we'll try with tongue too'.[18] The delicate song that follows upon this brutal bawdy is quite unrelated either to Cloten's purpose, to his nature, or to the tone of the scene:

> Hark, hark, the lark at heaven's gate sings,
>   and Phoebus gins arise,
> [His steeds to water at those springs
>   on chalic'd flowers that lies;]
> And winking Mary-buds begin to ope their golden eyes;
> With every thing that pretty is, my lady sweet arise:
>   Arise, arise!   (II.iii.14–26)

The disproportion of language to situation is at its most acute in that notorious scene where Imogen revives beside what she takes to be the headless body of her husband, though in fact it is Cloten in the clothes of Posthumus:

> . . . faith, I'll lie down and sleep.
>
> (*Seeing the body of Cloten*
>
> But soft! no bedfellow! O gods and goddesses!
> These flowers are like the pleasures of the world;
> This bloody man, the care on't . . .
> A headless man? The garments of Posthumus?
> I know the shape of 's leg: this is his hand:
> His foot Mercurial: his Martial thigh:

[17] For music and commentary see J.M. Nosworthy (ed.), *Cymbeline* (London, 1955), pp. 220–2. The passage within square brackets was not set in the Bodleian manuscript. It is unclear whether Cloten is intended to join his voice with the professional singer (see l.15) or not, and it must remain uncertain whether the first performance used this setting or another. The words clearly demand the kind of setting that is extant.

[18] References are to the Arden edition of *Cymbeline*, ed. J.M. Nosworthy (London, 1955).

The brawns of Hercules: but his Jovial face—
Murder in heaven! How?—'Tis gone. Pisanio,
All curses madded Hecuba gave the Greeks,
And mine to boot, be darted on thee! Thou,
Conspir'd with that irregulous devil, Cloten,
Hath here cut off my lord. To write and read
Be henceforth treacherous! Damn'd Pisanio
Hath with his forged letters (damn'd Pisanio)
From this most bravest vessel of the world
Struck the main-top! O Posthumus, alas!
Where is thy head? where's that? Ay me! where's that?
Pisanio might have kill'd thee at the heart,
And left this head on.   (IV.ii.294–323)

Consider the technical problems confronting a boy actor who
attempts to play Imogen as though she were Swinburne's matchless
heroine. Throughout the scene, he must simulate an extravagant
sorrow and yet be denied the full empathy of his audience, who are
watching a performance of grief that they know to be misplaced.
Initially, he has to negotiate the lines 'Faith, I'll lie down and sleep./
But soft! no bedfellow!' without raising a titter at the lady's
misapprehending prissiness. Next comes some fatuous and
inopportune moralizing over the flowers on the corpse: 'These
flowers are like the pleasures of the world; / This bloody man, the
care on't.' A little later, hoping that his audience will not be amused
at the way Shakespeare upends the old cliché 'That's my husband, I'd
know him anywhere', the actor has to cope with the crescendo 'this
is his hand: / His foot Mercurial: his Martial thigh: / The brawns of
Hercules', right up to the climactic pun 'but his Jovial face'—and
then get away with a literalist application of 'Jovial': 'Murder in
heaven!' The pun on 'Jovial' is inescapable, for 'jovy' meaning
'jovial, merry' was current at least by 1426, and Drayton's use of
'jovial' in the modern sense is recorded by *The Oxford English
Dictionary* eight years before the same author's use of it in the more
restricted meaning of 'Jove-like', 'imperial'. In sequence, the boy-
Imogen must then vent an extravagant sentiment that requires
reading and writing to be regarded henceforward as treacherous, he
must follow it with a fanciful metaphor that compares Posthumus to
a ship from which the main topmast has been lopped, and then make
thrice-repeated request to know the location of the absent head. He

concludes with a quibble against Pisanio for preferring decapitation to stabbing to the heart.[19]

A dramatist learns early not to set traps like these for his actors, unless by design. They cannot easily be attributed to an inept collaborator, for throughout the play unavoidably comic effects are interspersed among passages of great beauty and psychological truth. The simplest effect is one of deflation. Pisanio, wild-eyed and sighing, informs Imogen of his master's command to kill her and protests his own reluctance:

> O gracious lady:
> Since I received command to do this business
> I have not slept one wink.

But his rhetoric gets short shrift from Imogen:

> Do't, and to bed then.
>   (III.iv.99–101)

Again, Cornelius's announcement at Act V, scene v of the death of Cymbeline's Queen is deflated by Cymbeline's apparently overriding need to score points off the medical profession:

> Who worse than a physician
> Would this report become? But I consider,
> By med'cine life may be prolong'd, yet death
> Will seize the doctor too.   (V.v.27–30)

Almost as easy to pick up is the comedy of deliberate excess. Imogen regrets she could not take leave of Posthumus, for she 'had / Most pretty things to say' (I.iv.25–6); but she and Pisanio make up for it by some thirty-seven lines of 'pretty things' on the

---

[19] John Russell Brown feels that the comedy of the speech 'is entirely subdued, becoming part of the terror of Imogen's nightmare-dream' as she surfaces from drugged sleep, but observes that 'the apparent reality . . . is so absurd that very few actresses have dared to use all the words provided'. Bernard Shaw, though he believed Shakespeare had successfully created a 'dim half-asleep funny state of consciousness', nevertheless found himself unable to understand what 'A headless man' was doing in the text and advised Ellen Terry to cut that phrase from her performance. That excisions are made by actors who wish to play the lines for simple pathos suggests to me that they are cutting across Shakespeare's intention. (See J.R. Brown, *Shakespeare's Plays in Performance* (London, 1966), pp. 107–8).

circumstances of Posthumus's departure. Earlier, Posthumus, in informing Imogen of his *poste restante* address for letters, had given an old cliché a sudden and literalist turn:

> thither write, my queen,
> And with my eyes I'll drink the words you send,
> Though ink be made of gall.   (I.ii.30–2)

But other effects require from us a more delicate and responsive ear. There is the self-mocking preciosity of Guiderius's lament over Imogen/Fidele:

> Why, he but sleeps:
> If he be gone, he'll make his grave a bed:
> *With female fairies will his tomb be haunted*,
> And worms will not come to thee.
>   (IV.ii.215–18; italics added)

But this shades off into a more purely decorative yet moving response from Arviragus:

> With fairest flowers,
> Whilst summer lasts, and I live here, Fidele,
> I'll sweeten thy sad grave: thou shalt not lack
> The flower that's like thy face, pale primrose, nor
> The azur'd harebell, like thy veins: no, nor
> The leaf of eglantine, whom not to slander,
> Outsweet'ned not thy breath . . .   (IV.ii.218–24)

And yet that itself is undercut by Guiderius's interruption to protest against playing 'in wench-like words with that / Which is so serious' (229–31).

   A more sophisticated effect yet is the self-admiring preciosity that solicits for its extravagance the audience's amused attention. When Iachimo observes the crucial mole on Imogen's breast, 'a mole cinque-spotted: like the crimson drops / I' th' bottom of a cowslip' (II.ii.37–9), we are asked to admire the virtuosity of an artist whose flower comparisons are equal to any occasion. Such effects are not uncommon in the play, and move a connoisseur of language not so much to mirth as to amused delight. Often, Shakespeare aims at a bravura display that calls to mind Dryden's comment on Shaftesbury who 'Would steer too nigh the sands to boast his wit'—

the conceits stop just short of disaster, but only just. Imogen, baring
her breast to Pisanio's sword, discovers Posthumus's love-letters in
her bosom:

> Come, here's my heart,
> (Something's afore't,—soft, soft! we'll no defence)
> Obedient as the scabbard. What is here?
> The scriptures of the loyal Leonatus,
> All turn'd to heresy? Away, away,
> Corrupters of my faith! You shall no more
> Be stomachers to my heart: thus may poor fools
> Believe false teachers.   (III.iv.78–85)

Earlier in the same scene, Pisanio shows Imogen the letter accusing
her of whoredom, and his aside steers so near the rocks because the
paradoxical metaphor could almost literally be true:

> What shall I need to draw my sword? the paper
> Hath cut her throat already.   (III.iv.32–3)

The effect of such lines has of course to be pointed by the actor, and
insensitive playing could mask the humour altogether. Granville-
Barker[20] thought actors might 'allow themselves a certain slight
sophistication of style for its delivery'. He observed that Iachimo
'presents us, in his arrogance, with an approach to a travesty of
himself, which is also a travesty of the very medium in which he
exists';[21] and the actor delivering himself of Iachimo's defence to
Imogen for attempting to seduce her must allow himself an Italianate
flourish, as he brings the old conceit of 'sifting' characters to an
elegant, revivified conclusion:

> Be not angry,
> Most mighty princess, that I have adventur'd
> To try your taking of a false report, which hath
> Honour'd with confirmation your great judgement
> In the election of a sir so rare,

[20] *Prefaces to Shakespeare*, I, p. 498.
[21] *Prefaces to Shakespeare*, I, p. 502. The copy text for *Cymbeline* is agreed
to have been either Shakespeare's holograph or a very faithful transcript
from it, so it is curious to find the New Cambridge editor commenting on
the Folio's 'elaborate and sometimes melodramatic punctuation' (p. 126).
Was the 'melodramatic' punctuation intended as a guide to performing
style?

> Which you know cannot err. The love I bear him
> Made me to fan you thus, but the gods made you
> (Unlike all others) *chaffless*. Pray, your pardon.
>
> (I. vi. 171–8; italics added)

This self-consciousness in language, ranging from deliberate deflation of Romance posturing through to virtuoso, bravura display, is paralleled in the action by a persistently humorous treatment of those clichés of Romance incident and theme that go to make up the plot. A play that has the Rome of Augustus contemporary with modern Italy, that clothes Cymbeline's court in the trappings of the Renaissance, and has most traffic between Britain and the Continent passing through Milford Haven, far outdoes the 'sea-coast of Bohemia' for characteristic Romance absurdity. The Romance elements of *Cymbeline*, like those burlesqued in *The Knight of the Burning Pestle*, have a general provenance that is more important than their particular source: if the plot of the 'Falsely Accused Wife' derives immediately from *The Decameron* and from *Frederyke of Jennen*, its analogues range throughout European literature, beginning with the early thirteenth-century *Guillame de Dole* by Jean Renart. That Shakespeare's play is compounded of cliché is signalled to us in Act I, scene i by the First Gentleman, who has explained how Cymbeline's sons were stolen in infancy, but finds the Second Gentleman incredulous:

> That a king's children should be so convey'd,
> So slackly guarded, and the search so slow
> That could not trace them!
> *First Gent.*   Howsoe'er 'tis strange,
> Or that the negligence may well be laugh'd at,
> Yet is it true, sir.   (I. i. 63–7)

Failure to protect young infants from theft is hardly risible in itself: it is only laugh-worthy as a corny beginning to a plot.

The presumption that royalty must shine through its rustic cladding, which Shakespeare treats seriously in the case of Perdita in *The Winter's Tale*, is in *Cymbeline* chiefly a target for mockery. In darkest Wales Belarius, moralizing *ad nauseam* 'from all things we see' (III. iii. 18), conducts the lost princes through a favourite Romance debate that weighs the merits of the active as against the contemplative life. The young savages' preference for action evokes

a soliloquy on the theme of 'blue blood will out'—but Belarius's
soliloquy is rudely punctured:

>   O thou goddess,
> Thou divine Nature; thou thyself thou blazon'st
> In these two princely boys: they are as gentle
> As zephyrs blowing below the violet,
> Not wagging his sweet head; and yet, as rough,
> (Their royal blood enchaf'd) as the rud'st wind
> That by the top doth take the mountain pine
> And make him stoop to th' vale. 'Tis wonder
> That an invisible instinct should frame them
> To royalty unlearn'd, honour untaught,
> Civility not seen from other, valour
> That wildly grows in them, but yields a crop
> As if it had been sow'd . . .

>   *Re-enter* GUIDERIUS.

> *Gui.*   Where's my brother?
> I have sent Cloten's clotpoll down the stream,
> In embassy to his mother; his body's hostage
> For his return.   (IV.ii.169–86)

The clichés of Romance plotting and characterization are exposed
for our mirth. Imogen, like Rosalind and a dozen other Romance
heroines, must disguise as a boy and undertake a journey. Pisanio, as
the ever-faithful stage servant, keeps the necessary equipment to
hand: *item*, one boy's suit suitable for princesses to disguise in. He
may appear troubled by the command to kill Imogen, he may
suggest to her a return to Court; but when she falls into the notion of
a journey and accepts the necessity of disguising her sex, he suddenly
produces the necessary props from behind his back:

> Forethinking this, I have already fit
> ('Tis in my cloak-bag) doublet, hat, hose, all
> That answer to them.   (III.iv.169–71)

We again find this effortless sliding into time-honoured Romance
roles when Imogen is discovered by the Roman Lucius. Though she
has just swooned over what she takes to be the headless body of her
husband, it takes a mere twenty-one lines for her to agree to be taken
into the service of Lucius as page-boy, otherwise as heroine
disguised. There is no attempt to make the decision psychologically

plausible; and though no play by Shakespeare lacks touches of life, it is generally true that the characters of *Cymbeline* tend much more than those of *The Winter's Tale* or *The Tempest* to be recognizable Romance types—the Good Physician, the Faithful Servant, the Boorish Suitor, the Italianate Villain—and some are frankly, obtrusively conventional. The Queen as Wicked Step-Dame, with her confessional asides and a repertoire of evil if ineffectual plots, is straight out of melodrama, and presented for our amusement: she dies of frustrated malice, regretting that she had failed to carry out her intended iniquities, and her last-act confession as reported by Cornelius (V.v.31–61) contains one fact we knew—that she hated Imogen—and a deal more than we ought to have suspected—that she meant to poison the princess, that she had never loved Cymbeline himself, but had married his position, abhorred his person, and intended to poison him, after securing the adoption of her son as heir. But characters in *Cymbeline* less stereotyped than the Wicked Queen fall easily into cliché: when the wrongly jealous Posthumus rants against the evils of woman, he is laughable in his excess of traditional denunciation. He regrets that women must have a half-share in the begetting of men, for this necessitates that men be bastards; he longs to isolate the woman's part in himself, since every human fault is attributable to women; he declares that their proverbial changeability extends to a rapid turnover of vices; and in conclusion he will 'write against them,/ Detest them, curse them' (II.iv.183–4).

I hardly dare to take on Swinburne and the worshippers of Imogen by extending the analysis of send-up into that characterization, except to note that Imogen has on occasion an English prissiness that the Victorians would have admired. Hearing from Iachimo a spirited account of Posthumus's supposed antics with Italian whores, she observes finally 'My lord, I fear / Has forgot Britain' (I.vii.112–13). She is given to ornamenting an occasion with 'pretty things', with sentimental or sententious utterances: opening a letter from Posthumus, she will apologize to the wax:

> Good wax, thy leave: blest be
> You bees that make these locks of counsel! Lovers
> And men in dangerous bonds pray not alike:
> Though forfeiters you cast in prison, yet
> You clasp young Cupid's tables.   (III.ii.35–9)

In this trait of irrelevant reflection or high-minded but inopportune moralizing Imogen is characteristic of many of the characters in the play. Granville-Barker asked of Pisanio 'Is [he] so confirmed a moralizer that, even though Imogen be stupent with horror at the accusation of adultery, he (and his author) must keep her standing there while he informs us that

>   'tis slander,
> Whose edge is sharper than the sword, whose tongue
> Outvenoms all the worms of Nile, whose breath
> Rides on the posting winds and doth belie—
> All corners of the world—kings, queens and states,
> Maids, matrons; nay, the secrets of the grave
> This viperous slander enters.'?[22]

The answer must be that he *is* a moralizer—once again, it is the clichés of Romance that are being mocked, that tendency of characters to moralize on the situation of themselves and others which marks the form from *The Arcadia* to *Mucedorus*, but which, as Professor Felperin has observed,[23] is not a feature of Shakespeare's style before that deliberately archaic Romance play, *Pericles*. In *The Winter's Tale* and *The Tempest* such moralizing elements are much reduced and are made relevant to character and situation, but in *Cymbeline* characters vent improving sentiments in season and out of season.

As yet there has been no mention of the plot of *Cymbeline*, which is interwoven like many traditional Romances from at least four disparate strands of action, but is brought together in a final dénouement that outdoes all other dénouements. An audience is already in possession of the necessary facts, so that its attention is focused on the art of the dramatist in placing all the elements in his final frame. The pieces lock in thick and fast, there are approximately twenty-four different revelations, so that Cymbeline cries at one point 'Does the world go round?' whilst Posthumus asks 'How come these staggers on me?' and Imogen passes out cold (V.v.229–32). The carpentry is so well done that Shakespeare can allow himself a little studied naïvety to highlight his skill. Dr Cornelius suddenly recalls an item he had overlooked in his rehearsal a couple of hundred lines before of the Wicked Queen's confession:

---

[22] *Prefaces to Shakespeare*, I, p. 499.
[23] Howard Felperin, *Shakespearean Romance* (Princeton, 1972), p. 151.

O gods!
I left out one thing which the Queen confess'd . . .
(V.v.243–4)

The mockery of neat-ended stories is compounded by Cymbeline's
fatuous bewilderment as he recovers three lost children in as many
minutes:

O, what am I!
A mother to the birth of three?   (V.v.369–70)

I would be happier with the argument that *Cymbeline* is an
extended mockery of the Romance form if it were possible to point
to some specific targets of satire, though it is true that Sheridan's
Critic, Stoppard's *The Real Inspector Hound*, and even Beaumont's
Knight of the Burning Pestle guy the characteristics of a genre far more
than they parody particular works. The dreadful fourteeners of the
Masque of Jupiter (V.iv) may echo the abysmal verse for divine
manifestations in old plays like *Clyomon and Clamydes* (1570–83) or
The Rare Triumphs of Love and Fortune (1589), and the details of
Jupiter's descent, 'in thunder and lightning, sitting upon an eagle',
throwing a thunderbolt (V.iv.92.s.d.), might mirror some
contemporary masque or show, for a design exists at Chatsworth for
Jonson's masque of *Tempe Restored* in 1632 which presents Jupiter
exactly thus.[24] The one precise allusion of which I feel confident is
the frequent and fulsome reference in the play to Milford Haven, a
deepwater harbour in Wales on the route from Ireland, but elevated
in *Cymbeline* to being the main seaport for the Continent.
Everything seems to happen around Milford Haven. Imogen cajoles
Pisanio to

say, and speak thick,
(Love's counsellor should fill the bores of hearing
To th' smothering of the sense) how far it is
To this same blessed Milford. And by th' way
Tell me how Wales was made so happy as
T' inherit such a haven.   (III.ii.57–62)

[24] Allardyce Nicoll, *Stuart Masques and the Renaissance Stage* (New York:
Blom reprint, 1963, of 1938 edition), Fig. 45, p. 94.

There was no town at Milford in Shakespeare's day, and the harbour was famous only as the landing-point of Henry Tudor on his way to overthrow Richard III and to establish the Tudor dynasty. It is likely that *Cymbeline* was first performed as part of the celebrations that marked the investiture of Prince Henry as Prince of Wales in June 1610.[25] During these festivities, Daniel's masque *Tethys' Festival* had introduced the Queen herself as Tethys, ushering in four ladies of the Court who represented four Welsh rivers that discharged into Milford Haven:

> All these within the goodly spacious Bay
> Of manifold inharboring *Milford* meetes;
> The happy Port of Vnion, which gaue way
> To that great Hero *HENRY*, and his fleete.
> To make the blest coniunction that begat
> O greater, and more glorious far then that.
>
> (11. 147–52)[26]

My guess is that, by the time *Cymbeline* was performed, the Court was ready to hoot with laughter at any further bowing and scraping in the direction of Welsh ports.

Such laughter of course need not imply that an audience was moved to scorn. Emrys Jones[27] has argued persuasively that *Cymbeline* is a work of panegyric, relating an ancient British king, who was distinguished chiefly by good relations with Augustus and by having reigned through the general *pax Romana* that surrounded the birth of Christ, to a new British king, James the self-styled 'Peacemaker', who united Britain once more and pacified Europe. References to Milford Haven in the play would be construed as a compliment to the King, who was (as panegyrists were eager to remind their audience) the great-grandson of Henry Tudor. I would wish only to emphasize that panegyric need not be poker-faced, any more than parody needs to be contemptuous. Affectionate fun poked at allusions which had been bandied about during the festivities that accompanied Henry's investiture is matched in the

[25] See G. Bullough, *Narrative and Dramatic Sources of Shakespeare*, 8 vols. (London, 1957–75), VIII, 11–12.
[26] Samuel Daniel, *The Complete Works*, ed. A.B. Grosart, 5 vols. (New York: Russell & Russell, 1973, first published 1885–96), III.314.
[27] Emrys Jones, 'Stuart *Cymbeline*', *Essays in Criticism*, 11 (1961), pp. 84–99.

plot by humorous mockery of the Romance form that Court and dramatist so much enjoyed.

That the literary targets for satire are general rather than particular permits humorous effects of a special kind. For example, the 'trunk episode' does have a direct source in *The Decameron*, but more important for the play is its wide provenance in versions such as *Frederyke of Jennen*. Iachimo takes Imogen through a classic seduction-routine, first accusing her husband of infidelity, then inviting her to revenge herself by adultery. When she is offended, he slips effortlessly into the equally familiar defence that he has attempted her chastity only to test her loyalty to his valued friend. Imogen is immediately appeased, inviting him to 'take my pow'r i' th' court for yours' (I.vii.179); and a few lines later she is agreeing to accommodate Iachimo's very large trunk in her bedroom. The pleasure for the audience is in watching a heroine so innocent and so ancient a Briton that she has never heard of the dangers of going to see a gentleman's etchings or of having 'some madeira, m'dear'.

If *Cymbeline* is really a send-up of the Romance form, there is little point in grouping it with *Pericles*, *The Winter's Tale*, and *The Tempest*. What it shares with those plays is merely the common material of Romance. Professor Felperin has done us a service by emphasizing that themes of rebirth, of regeneration through suffering, of reconciliation, redeeming time and the 'fortunate fall' are not invented by Shakespeare but are already there in the tradition.[28] It is not enough to call Act V of *Cymbeline*, as A.C. Kirsch has done, 'a sustained finale of rebirths':[29] the degree of seriousness in the handling is what matters. The limited contrition of Posthumus, the easy repentance of Iachimo, and the even greater ease with which he is forgiven, all those problems that have troubled serious critics, are signs that this Romance story does not aspire to rise above the commonplace. The reconciliations are deliberately perfunctory: though Cymbeline has spilt his country's blood in resisting Rome, and is still defiant when the last scene opens, the quarrel is hastily resolved by Cymbeline's admission that it was the Wicked Queen and Cloten who had seduced him into refusing tribute. The father-daughter relationship is of major importance in the three serious Late Romances of Shakespeare, and the restoration

---

[28] Felperin, *Shakespearean Romance*, *passim*.
[29] A.C. Kirsch, '*Cymbeline* and Coterie Dramaturgy', *English Literary History*, 34 (1967), pp. 285–306, an otherwise thought-provoking study.

of a lost daughter is climactic in two of them; but in *Cymbeline* the king is a cipher, the relationship with his daughter is barely sketched, and the return of Imogen to her father matters little more than the restoration of the lost prince and princess to their respective parents at the end of *Mucedorus*.

So it is with themes of providential control or of the 'fortunate fall': context and treatment are all-important. Characters in *Cymbeline* are given to expressions of piety or of vacuous optimism at unlikely moments: 'Heaven mend all!' exclaims Cymbeline (V.v.68) at the discovery that his Queen has never loved him and has plotted to poison him. Lucius, having (as he believes) dispatched Fidele's headless master for burial and found the lad a new position, offers a little quasi-Christian consolation:

> Be cheerful; wipe thine eyes:
> Some falls are means the happier to arise. (IV.ii.402–3)

Such jingles employed to end a scene are surely a mockery of the easy pieties of traditional Romance.

Jupiter's lines in the Masque

> Whom best I love I cross; to make my gift,
> The more delayed, delighted. Be content. (V.iv.101–2)

with their obvious scriptural reference would in another play demand to be taken seriously; here, they occur in a context of doggerel verse, as a declaration of providential care that comes too late in the play to comfort, and serves chiefly to provide a redundant oracle. In *The Winter's Tale* the oracle at Delphos serves an important dramatic function, for it declares Hermione to be innocent, and so asserts the possibility of right knowledge through contact with the controlling powers, even if Leontes may choose to set aside their revelation. In *Cymbeline*, the book dropped beside the sleeping Posthumus is remembered only after all has come out and the reconciliations have been made: the Soothsayer steps forward to exercise his ingenuity in squaring the prophecy with the facts, and the oracle becomes a hilarious coda to the whole piece:

> Thou, Leonatus, art the lion's whelp,
> The fit and apt construction of thy name,
> Being Leo-natus, doth impart so much:
> *(To Cymbeline)* The piece of tender air, thy virtuous daughter,

Which we call *mollis aer*; and *mollis aer*
We term it *mulier*: which *mulier* I divine
Is this most constant wife, who even now
Answering the letter of the oracle,
Unknown to you, unsought, were clipp'd about
With this most tender air.   (V.v.444–53)

'This hath some seeming', cries Cymbeline.

The suggestion that there is an element of self-parody in the execution of *Cymbeline* is not new, though I know of no one who has argued it to be so extensive. Frank Kermode felt Shakespeare was 'somehow *playing* with the play',[30] and J.C. Maxwell[31] believed that 'deliberate incongruity and comic exploitation of conventions' were carried even further than Harley Granville-Barker had suggested. Interestingly, it is those who like Granville-Barker have been intimately involved in performances of the play who have been most conscious of the parodic elements:[32] my own reading of *Cymbeline* derives from a production in December 1970 staged by my pupils at St John's College, Cambridge, in defiance of my contention that the play was unactable. In the course of a week's playing, they found that *Cymbeline* dictated to them an acting-style that might be called 'high camp': a conscious naïvety and studied exaggeration, where the actor observes himself playing beside his part. Terms such as parody or burlesque are unsatisfactory to describe the effect, for the play offers affectionate mockery of the Romance form, together with the delight of returning (as an amused sophisticate) to the pleasures of a less sophisticated youth. An age which has seen *Superman* or sat through the musical *The Boy Friend* is well placed to understand *Cymbeline*. The old pleasures have not simply gone: a degree of involvement in the story, a degree of seriousness, is permissible. The violence of Posthumus's jealousy is disturbing,

---

[30] Frank Kermode, *Shakespeare: The Final Plays*, Writers and their Work, 155 (London, 1963), p. 22.

[31] *Cymbeline*, ed. J.C. Maxwell (Cambridge, 1966), p. xxxix.

[32] J.R. Brown, for instance ('Playing for Laughs: the Last Plays', in his *Shakespeare's Plays in Performance*, pp. 91–112), insists that 'in *Cymbeline* the humour is dispersed throughout the action . . . the laughter that will undoubtedly come during rehearsals must be prized and its occasions carefully retained and possibly augmented in order to help present the delight and fantasy of the happy ending'. Nevertheless, Brown would find 'comedy and affecting dramatic narrative' mingled in more nearly equal proportions than I am here suggesting.

though he will relieve it by writing against women; Imogen's reaction to the false accusation moves us, even if she soon slips into a tirade against faithless men that is as foolish in its way as Posthumus's excesses.[33] It is the degree of genuine affection for the Romance form that distinguishes the art of *Cymbeline* from Kirsch's 'Coterie Dramaturgy'—there is nothing of Marston's sour mockery of himself and of his art.

My conclusion as to the nature of *Cymbeline* can only be a suggestion: because so much of the context that would clearly indicate humour has perished beyond recall, the suggestion (even more than most literary opinions) is incapable of proof. I am convinced that the Late Plays as a body provide the wrong context for understanding *Cymbeline*. There you have a serious use of Romance for special artistic purposes, perhaps the consequence of a development in Shakespeare's attitude to his art that made him unwilling to pretend any more to 'hold the mirror up to nature', and inclined him at most to offer an embroidered tapestry, a silk screen. I suspect that *Cymbeline* may be a sport, a unique creation, in reaction to criticisms of the Romance form by Jonson and his party, and perhaps suggested by the Court revival of *Mucedorus*. Maybe it is significant that *Cymbeline* is the only one of the four Late Romances that Jonson does not seem to have criticized. At the least, perhaps we could give up treating *Cymbeline* as a tin of sardines, with that little bit in the corner that we can't get out.

---

[33] On a lower level, the verbal defences of England by Cloten and the Queen are both a send-up of jingoist sentiment (Cloten's phrase about the 'salt-water girdle', III.i.82, comes close to John of Gaunt's famous speech) *and* a patriotic effusion which everyone in the audience can enjoy—as when the Demon King in pantomime pulls out a Union Jack and gives us a rousing chorus of 'Rule Britannia'.

III

Jonson's Magic Houses

IAN DONALDSON

I

The analogies which a writer uses to describe his art can often be revealing. For Ben Jonson the activity of writing was like that of building. A writer assembled words into a sentence as a builder put stones together to form a wall. 'The congruent, and harmonious fitting of parts in a sentence, hath almost the fastning, and force of knitting, and connexion', Jonson wrote in *Discoveries*, 'As in stones well squar'd, which will rise strong a great way without mortar' (ll. 1976–80).[1] What a writer finally created was an object like a house. Its various parts should be

> so joyn'd, and knitt together, as nothing in the structure can be chang'd, or taken away, without impairing, or troubling the whole; of which there is a proportionate magnitude in the members. As for example; if a man would build a house, he would first appoint a place to build it in, which he would define within certaine bounds: So in the Constitution of a *Poeme*, the Action is aym'd at by the *Poet*, which answers Place in a building; and that Action hath his largenesse, compasse, and proportion.
> (*Discoveries*, ll. 2683–91)

Literary works vary in scale and magnitude, as do different kinds of building: 'a Court, or King's Palace, requires other dimensions then a private house'. The various parts come together to form a whole 'as a house, consisting of diverse materialls, becomes one structure, and one dwelling'. Episodes and digressions 'are the same that household stuffe and other furniture are in a house' (*Discoveries*, ll. 2691–2,

---

[1] Quotations from *Ben Jonson*, ed. C.H. Herford and P. and E. Simpson, 11 vols. (Oxford, 1925–52); u/v and i/j regularized.

2791–2, 2748–9). The analogies are traditional,[2] yet at the same time
congenial to Jonson's creative imagination. It is characteristic of
Jonson to perceive literary works in spatial terms: as objects laid out
and built up like courts or palaces or private houses, to be walked
around, observed, inhabited, their details and proportions and
relationship of parts appreciatively assessed. And it is equally
characteristic of Jonson to speak of literary works as objects which
are consciously, solidly, monumentally constructed: built to last. To
the Lord Treasurer, Richard Weston, Earl of Portland, Jonson
writes:

> . . . though I cannot as an Architect
>   In glorious Piles, or Pyramids erect
> Unto your honour: I can tune in song
>   Aloud; and (happly) it may last as long.
>   (*The Underwood*, lxxvii.25–8)

'Architect' (the profession of Inigo Jones) is a word which Jonson
elsewhere utters with hostility or contempt, but 'glorious' here
concedes a counter-truth.[3] Architect and poet, it is tacitly admitted,
may have certain aims and functions in common; each is concerned
with construction and commemoration, and, up to a point, the
terminology of the one art may be equably appropriated for the
other.

However suggestive the analogy may have been for Jonson, it also
had its limits. It was not altogether a happy coincidence that Jonson
himself had actually worked as a builder in the early 1590s. From
time to time his enemies drew unkind comparisons between his past
and present occupations. Jonson is 'the wittiest fellow of a Bricklayer
in England', declares one character dryly in the second part of *The
Return From Parnassus*, and his companion at once takes up the cue: he
is 'so slow an Inventor, that he were better betake himself to his old

---

[2] Jonson is following Vives, *De Ratione Dicendi*, bk. i, 1555, and Heinsius,
De Tragoediae Constitutione, 1611: Heinsius is in turn following Aristotle,
Poetics, ch. vii and viii (where these analogies are not, however, to be found).
Cf. Congreve's epistle to Charles Mountague, on *The Double Dealer*: 'the
Mechanical part of it is perfect. That, I may say with as little vanity, as a
Builder may say he has built a House according to the Model laid down
before him; or a Gardiner that he has set his Flowers in a knot of such or such
a Figure': *Complete Plays of William Congreve*, ed. Herbert Davis (Chicago
and London, 1967), pp. 118–19.
[3] 'Architect': *Epigrams*, cxv. 30; cf. *Ungathered Verse*, xxxiv.37.

trade of Bricklaying; a bould whorson, as confident now in making of a booke, as he was in times past in laying of a brick'.[4] Making a book, laying a brick: put the two activities so humorously together, and the analogy itself at once becomes absurd; Jonson is seen as an intellectual navvy, a thoughtless wielder of flat heavy objects. Modern readers, nurtured on Romantic images of organic form, are likely to be especially sensitive to the limitations of the analogy between writing and building. Leavis's famous comment about Milton comes to mind: 'a good deal of *Paradise Lost* strikes one as being almost as mechanical as bricklaying'.[5] Nineteenth-century critics were wont to allude with routine distaste to Jonson's early career as a manual labourer. For Carlyle, Jonson was 'the rugged Stonemason, the harsh, learned Hodman'; for Macaulay, 'Ben's heroic couplets resemble blocks rudely hewn out by an unpractised hand, with a blunt hatchet.'[6] Felix Schelling put the matter succinctly: 'We cannot expect the laws which govern organic growth to coincide with those controlling constructive ingenuity; a house is built, a tree grows, and the conscious and self-controlled development of such a man as Jonson is alien to the subtle and harmonious unfolding of a genius like Shakespeare's'.[7]

'A house is built, a tree grows': the distinction is a telling one, but it is a distinction which Jonson himself might be said to have anticipated. His own collections of verse and prose are significantly entitled *The Forest, The Underwood, Timber,* and the promise which these titles offer—of spontaneous organic life, of multiform things 'promiscuously growing'—is as important to an understanding of Jonson's aesthetic as is the imagery of artisanship, labour, and

---

[4] *The Return From Parnassus*, Pt. II, I.ii.293–9, in *The Three Parnassus Plays (1598–1601)*, ed. J.B. Leishman (London, 1949), p. 244.

[5] F.R. Leavis, 'Milton's Verse', *Revaluation* (London, 1962), p. 60. For the background to this remark, and a more detailed account of the metaphors used in Jonsonian criticism, see Ian Donaldson, 'Damned by Analogies: Or, How to Get Rid of Ben Jonson', *Gambit, International Theatre Review*, vi (1972), 38–46. On the organic metaphor, see *Organic Form: The Life of an Idea*, ed. G.S. Rousseau (London, 1972).

[6] Thomas Carlyle, *Historical Sketches of Notable Persons and Events in the Reign of James I and Charles I* (London, n.d. [1898]), p. 74; Lord Macaulay, *Critical and Historical Essays Contributed to the Edinburgh Review* (London, 1878), p. 705.

[7] Felix E. Schelling, *Ben Jonson and the Classical School* (Baltimore, 1898), p. 24.

rational planning.[8] Building was in any case an art which Jonson regarded with wariness and suspicion. In 'An Expostulation with Inigo Jones' (*Ungathered Verse*, xxxiv) building is represented as the product and symbol of 'the money-gett, Mechanick Age' (l. 52); it trades merely in externals—in painting and carpentry, cloth and deal-board for the court masque, in 'Purbeck stone' for the new Banqueting House at Whitehall—lacking the life and 'soul' which poetry can impart.[9]

Jonson's animus against building is also apparent in 'To Penshurst' (*The Forest*, ii). It is Penshurst's praise that it has not been 'built to envious show' in the manner of other ostentatious houses of the day, but stands, 'an ancient pile', as though rooted in the grounds from time immemorial.[10] The point is made another way in the poem's concluding lines:

> Now, PENSHURST, they that will proportion thee
> With other edifices, when they see
> Those proud, ambitious heaps, and nothing else,
> May say, their lords have built, but thy lord dwells.
>
> (ll. 99–102)

Building in itself is nothing: what matters is the life that animates a building. Though remarkably precise in its physical and topographical detail, Jonson's poem is not essentially concerned with the bricks and stones and mortar of Penshurst, but with the kind of life that the *house*, in its fullest sense—a dynasty and a

---

[8] On the arboreal metaphor, see in particular Alastair Fowler, 'The Silva Tradition in Jonson's *The Forest*', in *Poetic Traditions of the English Renaissance*, ed. Maynard Mack and George deForest Lord (New Haven and London, 1982), pp. 163–80. 'Promiscuously growing': see 'To the Reader', prefixed to *The Underwood*.

[9] See D.J. Gordon, 'Poet and Architect: The Intellectual Setting of the Quarrel Between Ben Jonson and Inigo Jones', *Journal of the Warburg and Courtauld Institutes*, 12 (1949), 152–78; Stephen Orgel, Introduction to *The Complete Masques of Ben Jonson* (New Haven, 1969); Stephen Orgel and Roy Strong, *Inigo Jones: The Theatre of the Stuart Court*, 2 vols. (London, Berkeley, and Los Angeles, 1973), *passim*.

[10] Penshurst was built about 1340, over two hundred years before the Sidney family came to live there. Jonson may be contrasting the antiquity of Penshurst with the brash modernity of such buildings as Knole and Theobalds. See G.R. Hibbard, 'The Country House Poem of the Seventeenth Century', *JWCI*, 19 (1956), pp. 159–74; Alastair Fowler, *Conceitful Thought* (Edinburgh, 1975), pp. 114–34.

household, an edifice and an estate—is capable of fostering and sustaining. 'Thy lord dwells': but as J.C.A. Rathmell has shown, it was an awkward fact that Lord Lisle, who was undergoing personal difficulties at the time when Jonson wrote this poem, did not in fact dwell at Penshurst as regularly and faithfully as he should have done.[11] The master of Penshurst plays a marginal role throughout Jonson's poem, despite the final tribute that is paid to him. One might contrast the way in which Jonson locates Lord Bacon centrally within York House, and centrally within his own birthday poem to him:

> Haile, happie *Genius* of this antient pile!
> How comes it all things so about thee smile?
> The fire, the wine, the men! and in the midst,
> Thou stand'st as if some Mysterie thou did'st!
>
> (*The Underwood*, li. 1–4)

The central character within 'To Penshurst' is instead Penshurst itself, which is at once the subject and the recipient of the poem. Penshurst is imbued with a life and consciousness of its own. Jonson speaks to the house with tenderness:

> Nor, when I take my lodging, need I pray
> For fire, or lights, or livorie: all is there;
> As if thou, then, wert mine, or I raign'd here . . .
>
> (ll. 72–7)

'As if thou, then, wert mine': the words might almost be uttered to a lover. In such a house, the guest feels like a king ('or I raign'd here'); and thus by a natural transition Jonson shifts to an account of the unexpected visit to Penshurst one night of King James and his son Prince Henry, who glimpsed the glow of fires from the windows of Penshurst while hunting in the nearby woods.

> What (great, I will not say, but) sodayne cheare
> Did'st thou, then, make 'hem! and what praise was heap'd
> On thy good lady, then! who, therein, reap'd
> The just reward of her high huswifery;
> To have her linnen, plate, and all things nigh,
> When she was farre: and not a roome, but drest,
> As if it had expected such a guest!   (ll. 82–8)

[11] J.C.A. Rathmell, 'Jonson, Lord Lisle, and Penshurst', *ELR*, 1 (1971), pp. 250–60.

Who looked after the royal party? Though Jonson tactfully praises the forethought of Lady Lisle, he also makes it clear that she and her husband were actually not at home when the king and his son chanced by. The king and his entourage, the poem wittily suggests, were cared for by *the house itself*, which made them 'sodayne cheare'. 'Not a roome, but drest,/ As if it had expected such a guest!': '*drest*' (the word is aptly and humorously chosen for its double reference) as a person might be dressed; each room thoughtfully 'expected such a guest'. By these and other similar touches throughout the poem, Jonson creates a sense of Penshurst as a kind of magic house, animated and sentient, with a mind and will and influence all of its own: expectant, beneficent, welcoming, enabling.

Jonson elsewhere writes of other buildings which are magically animated. As King James entered the city of London in 1603, Jonson declared in the *Panegyre* he had written to welcome him, 'every windore griev'd it could not move / Along with him' (ll. 45–6).

> All the aire was rent,
> As with the murmure of a moving wood;
> The ground beneath did seeme a moving floud:
> Walls, windores, roofes, towers, steeples, all were set
> With severall eyes, that in this object met.   (ll. 60–4)

The eyes seem to belong not to the city's inhabitants, but to the city itself, straining to glimpse its new monarch. Another house with a will of its own is that which expects the new bride Frances Stuart after her marriage to the Earl of Essex in the masque *Hymenaei*:

> Haste, tender *lady*, and adventer;
> The covetous *house* would have you enter,
>   That it might wealthy bee,
>   And you, her mistris see:
>   Haste your owne good to meet;
>   And lift your golden feet
>   Above the *threshold*, high,
>   With prosperous *augury*.   (ll. 477–84)

The trope of the animated house is less subtly developed in these two instances than in 'To Penshurst', but its imaginative possibilities are none the less apparent.

These possibilities Jonson was to exploit most fully not in the court masque (despite the opportunities for scenic transformation which the masque offered) nor in his non-dramatic poetry, but in his plays written for the public stage. And it is to these I want now to turn.

II

Part of Jonson's great power as a dramatist lies in his understanding of the pressures and excitements associated with confined spaces. No dramatist before him (and none after, until recent times) so fully explores the psychology of urban indoor living, so instinctively perceives the correspondence between the fixed space of a house and the fixed space of the stage on which actors must work. To think of a play by Jonson is to think at once of the house in which its action occurs. There is Morose's house in *The Silent Woman*, strategically situated in a lane too narrow to admit carts and coaches, its door quilted, its windows shut and caulked, its walls and ceilings doubly and trebly reinforced, its master living fearfully within by candlelight. There is Agrippina's house in *Sejanus* where the spies Opsius and Rufus stow themselves in their holes between the roof and ceiling in the hope of hearing seditious talk below. There is Corvino's house in *Volpone*, where the hapless Celia is confined, a chalk line drawn on the floor beyond which she must not stray, the window giving on to the Piazza—the 'publike windore' from which she has dropped her handkerchief to the supposed mountebank Scoto of Mantua—closed off: 'I will have this bawdy light dam'd up' (II.v.3, 50). And there is that mysterious, enticing house where the Magnifico himself apparently lies dying: a house to which each of the legacy-hunters in turn is irresistibly drawn and which each wishes dearly to possess; a house from which Volpone himself is in the end excluded by the skilful manoeuvrings of his own servant and seeming ally, Mosca. The idea of a man and his wealth confined to a house is imaginatively central to the play. (John Aubrey thought the character of Volpone was modelled on that of Captain Thomas Sutton, the financier, who ended his days 'in Fleetstreet at a Wollen draper's shop, opposite to Fetter-lane; where he had so many great Chests full of money, that his chamber was ready to groane under it, and Mr. Tyndall, who knew him . . ., was afrayd the roome would fall . . .).[12] The houses in Jonson's plays are

[12] *Aubrey's Brief Lives*, ed. O.L. Dick (London, 1960), p. 291. Jonson may also have remembered Barabas's 'Infinite riches in a little room', *The Jew of Malta*, I.i.37.

by turns comforting, protective, sinister, attractive. They are not merely 'settings': they are also in a deep symbolic sense what the plays are about.

The confined locations of Jonson's dramas can generate a high degree of stage excitement; they can also generate a range of psychological and metaphorical meaning. In *The Silent Woman*, Morose's obsessive concern with living alone and undisturbed in his own house ('Is the dore shut?', II.v.3) suggests a way of life entirely contrary to that which Jonson depicts at Penshurst, where 'all come in, the farmer and the clowne' to enjoy the 'open table' that the master of the house provides (ll. 48, 27). Morose's house offers no such hospitality: even his wedding breakfast must be forcibly brought into the house from outside, against his wishes. The revellers and tormentors violate his solitary and solipsistic way of life in a kind of parody of the sexual act that should rightfully consummate his wedding ('this horne got me entrance, kisse it', says Truewit, II.iv.10). The house in which Morose has shut himself remains a thing of bricks and mortar and quilted doors, lacking in life and vitality. Though Morose has chosen to marry, he will never establish (in a further, generational sense of the word) a house of his own: his wife, as the final, busy moments of the play reveal, is no woman and therefore no wife. Morose's own desperate confession of physical impotence, wrung from him in the seconds before this final revelation, is a fiction devised to secure his divorce, but it retains its symbolic appropriateness as a characterization of his total way of life, shut up within his own house. This way of life is contrasted with that of the absurdly 'open' man, Sir Amorous La Foole, whose *house* spills its progeny with disconcerting fecundity to all points of the compass: 'They all come out of our house, the LA-FOOLES o' the north, the LA-FOOLES of the west, the LA-FOOLES of the east, and south—we are as ancient a family, as any is in *Europe*' (I.iv.37–40). Literal and metaphorical meanings of the word 'house' play off against each other here, as so often elsewhere in Jonson's writing. The reckless disclosures of La Foole, who invites guests to plays and suppers 'aloud, out of his windore, as they ride by in coaches' (I.iii.34–5), is contrasted with the determined isolationism of Morose, who ensures that all his windows are closed up.

Corvino, another stopper-up of windows and social pleasures, forbids his wife a view over the Piazza yet grants her access to the house's rearward prospects; and himself, by process of Freudian association, one avenue of sexual gratification.

Then, here's a locke, which I will hang upon thee;
And, now I thinke on't, I will keepe thee backe-wards;
Thy lodging shall be backe-wards; thy walkes back-wards;
Thy prospect—all be backe-wards; and no pleasure,
That thou shalt know, but backe-wards . . .   (II.v.57–61)

To close off the windows at the front of the house and leave the back
ones open is entirely in character for Corvino, whose apparent
absolutism is never what it seems. His mind, like his house, is not
quite closed: through one loophole he will rashly argue his escape
from the mental fortress he has established, dragging his wife to the
very bedside of the man who most wishes to possess her. In *Sejanus*
(to offer one more instance of Jonson's suggestive trafficking
between the literal and the metaphorical) what those spies in
Agrippina's ceiling overhang is an entire dynasty and its fortunes,
not simply a physical structure. 'It is a noble constancie you shew/
To this afflicted house', says Latiaris to Sabinus as the spies crawl to
their crannies (IV.115–16), and the timing of his remark deftly
enlarges its symbolic sense. The simple stage action of the spies'
concealing themselves in the rafters of the house gives menacing
particularity to the larger affliction of which Latiaris speaks.[13] The
house already contains the elements of its own destruction.

Nowhere in his work, however, does Jonson more subtly explore
the tensions of domestic living, nowhere does he more skilfully
elaborate the manifold meanings of that seemingly simple concept, a
'house', than in his comic masterpiece, *The Alchemist*. No other
house which Jonson created more fully deserves the epithet '*magic*'
than that house in Blackfriars where three confidence workers ply
their trade.

III

The action of *The Alchemist* is played out within strict limits both
of time and of space. Though modern editions of the play sometimes
obscure this fact, the entire action, apart from the scenes in Act Five
in the lane outside the house, takes place within a single room of
Lovewit's house. There are rooms opening off this area—most

[13] See Francis Berry, 'Stage Perspective and Elevation in *Coriolanus* and
Sejanus', in *Jonson and Shakespeare*, ed. Ian Donaldson (London and Basing-
stoke, 1983), pp. 163–78.

notably, Subtle's laboratory, which (significantly and suggestively) is never fully revealed—and there are the rooms to which Mammon and the Spanish Count are permitted to retire for their amorous engagements. Somewhere 'within', too, is the privy into which the luckless Dapper is hurriedly stowed at a critical moment of the play, there to be forgotten. The acting area itself, however, is confined: no use is made of the inner rooms or upper stage for acting purposes, allowing for a concentration of effect which, as E.K. Chambers observed many years ago, is quite unprecedented in the English theatre.[14]

This sense of enclosure is important to the total effect of the play, generating for audience and characters alike various sensations of curiosity, nervousness, and claustrophobia. Lovewit's house in Blackfriars, like Volpone's house in Venice, serves as a 'honeypot', a 'center attractive', a powerful magnet to draw the curious and unwary; what goes on within the house is a constant source of speculation and fascination. The house itself serves as a trap: a trap that may also spring on the tricksters themselves, who (unlike Volpone and Mosca) have no legitimate claim to occupy the house and use it in the way they do. The house is set in a neighbourhood, and there is the constant risk that the activities of Dol, Subtle, and Face and their victims will be overheard or overlooked. The conspirators are nervous on this matter right from the start of the play, and in their more reckless and rebellious moments choose to provoke each other by raising their voices.

> *Dol*   Will you have
>   The neighbours heare you? Will you betray all?
>   . . .
> *Face*   Will you be so lowd?
>   . . .
> *Subtle*   I wish, you could advance your voice, a little.
>   . . .
> *Face*   You might talke softlier, raskall.
> *Subtle*   No, you *scarabe*,
>   I'll thunder you, in peeces.   (I.i.7–8, 18, 32, 59–60)

[14] E.K. Chambers, *The Elizabethan Stage*, 4 vols. (Oxford, 1923), III.123. Cf. W.A. Armstrong, 'Ben Jonson and Jacobean Stagecraft', in *Jacobean Theatre*, ed. John Russell Brown and Bernard Harris, Stratford-upon-Avon Studies, 1 (London, 1960), pp. 43–61, at p. 47.

Within the house, there is a similar fear of being overheard; it is as
though the walls were paper-thin. When Sir Epicure Mammon is
given his opportunity to court Dol Common, Face tells him that his
wooing is all too audible in the next room.

> Face Sir, you are too loud. I heare you, every word,
>   Into the laboratory. Some fitter place.
>   The garden, or great chamber above.   (IV.i.170–2)

During a later quarrel with Subtle, Face threatens to call out 'And
loose the hinges' (IV.iii.82) so Dol can know that Subtle, contrary to
the terms of the alliance, has designs upon Dame Pliant. A single cry
might suffice to destroy the conspiracy. At the beginning of Act
Five, a confused neighbour is to tell Lovewit that three weeks earlier
he heard 'a dolefull cry' emanating from the house while he sat up
mending his wife's stockings: 'like unto a man / That had beene
strangled an houre, and could not speake' (V.i.33, 36–7). Not long
afterwards, *Dapper cryes out within* (V.iii.63, s.d.), shattering the
fiction which Face has hastily devised to explain for Lovewit's
benefit what has been occurring in the house while he has been away.
The constant knocking at the door of the house heightens the sense
of nervous apprehension; it is not always at first clear whether a new
caller is friend or foe. 'Is he the Constable?' asks Kastril suspiciously
after the entrance of Ananias at IV.vii.44. In Act Five, the master
himself is seen knocking repeatedly at the door of his own house.
After his admission, the knocking continues, for later in the fifth act,
Mammon, Tribulation, Ananias, Surly, and Kastril return to the
house with Officers, noisily demanding entry. 'Harke you,
thunder', says Face to Subtle, coolly offering to him and to Dol a
means of escape from the trap that has now closed upon them:

>   All I can doe
> Is to helpe you over the wall, o' the back-side;
> Or lend you a sheet, to save your velvet gowne, DOL.
>   (V.iv.132–4)

By a variety of small touches, Jonson thus makes us acutely aware
of Lovewit's house as a potentially confining place: as a box or prison
within which the action of the comedy is played out. Dol spies from
the windows of the house, as from a loop-hole, into the lane outside,
and communicates with unwanted callers by means of a speaking
tube: 'Thorough the trunke, like one of your *familiars*', I.iv.5. At

moments of high excitement, Face and Subtle rebound within the house like balls within an enclosed court:

> *Face*   Let us be light, though.
> *Subtle*   I, as balls, and bound
> And hit our heads against the roofe for joy:
> There's so much of our care now cast away.   (IV.v.98–100)

The supposed Spanish don is lured, as though to a prison: fettered by Dol's fair looks, he is to be 'throwne/ In a downe-bed, as darke as any dungeon' (III.iii.41–3).

The fixed setting of *The Alchemist* also creates an air of mystery. What cannot be seen from outside the house or from the single room to which most of the visitors gain access is darkly guessed at. The house is constantly spoken of as something more than a house. Mammon fancifully pictures it as '*novo orbe*', 'the rich *Peru*', 'a meere *Chancell*' for Subtle's high art (II.i.2, V.iii.2). His companion, Surly, sceptically convinced that the place is nothing but a bawdy house, nevertheless aggrandizes it in his sterner denunciations, speaking gravely of 'The subtilties of this darke *labyrinth*' and of 'the knaveries of this *Citadell*' (II.iii.308, IV.vi.9).[15] For other visitors, the house is the residence of a 'cunning-man' (I.ii.8) who can advise them on many matters, a centre of social, religious, and alchemical mysteries. Abel Drugger, an ardent believer in the mystical significance of the art of building, visits the house in Blackfriars in order to consult with Subtle on the construction and disposition of the tobacconist shop which he is about to erect for himself. Subtle solemnly advises him of the most auspicious orientation for the shop, and urges him to bury a lode-stone beneath its threshold, 'To draw in gallants, that weare spurres: The rest,/ They'll seeme to follow' (I.iii.70–1)— advice that humorously reminds us of the magnetic effect that the house in which Subtle himself operates appears to exercise on those who visit it (Drugger himself has been drawn in, as if by the heels). The neighbours with whom Lovewit talks in the lane at the beginning of the fifth act cannot confidently say what has been going on within the house: whether and how it has been used, whether and by whom it has been visited, whether 'open house' has been maintained, or (as Face asserts) the doors have been securely locked

---

[15] Jonson's *Epigrams*, vii, 'On the New Hot-House', turns on a similar ambiguity concerning a building's actual nature and function.

for the past three weeks. 'We were deceiv'd, he sayes', admits one
neighbour, lamely (V.i.42). The house in Blackfriars is capable of
being whatever people most want it to be: it is a shell within which
their fantasies may be projected, a sounding board for the
imagination. When Lovewit finally enters the house, he finds it
strangely desolate and abandoned:

> Here, I find
> The emptie walls, worse then I left 'hem, smok'd,
> A few crack'd pots, and glasses, and a fornace,
> The seeling fill'd with *poesies* of the candle:
> And MADAME, with a *Dildo*, writ o' the walls.   (V.v.38–42)

For Ananias, on the other hand, this is not just an empty house: it is 'a
cage of uncleane birds', 'this den of theeves' (V.iii.47, V.v.93). Even
as he denounces the place, Ananias (like Surly) makes it sound
grander, more mysterious, more compelling, than Lovewit's sober
account has suggested. Ananias will go to Amsterdam:

> I will pray there,
> Against thy house: may dogs defile thy walls,
> And waspes, and hornets breed beneath thy roofe,
> This seat of false-hood, and this cave of cos'nage.   (V.v.112–15)

'Cage', 'den', 'seat', 'cave': this is no ordinary house, but a magical
place, a centre of spiritual enchantment.

The 'house' against which Ananias determines to direct his
vengeful prayers is the physical edifice in Blackfriars whose inner
rooms Ananias and his companions have now at last penetrated; it is
also the entire dynasty and household of Lovewit, which Ananias
believes to be responsible for the downfall and humiliation of the
Brethren. The 'house' of Lovewit at present comprises exactly three
people, Lovewit himself, his new wife Dame Pliant, and his servant
Jeremy, alias Face; Ananias's terrible curse aggrandizes the strength
of this house even as it threatens its destruction. The imagination
that can convert a common London dwelling house into a
Spenserian 'cave of cos'nage' can equally convert three people into
an Old Testament dynasty.

The comedy is much concerned with the creation of such
imaginary dynastic 'houses'. Sir Epicure Mammon, after catching a
subliminal glimpse of Dol Common, is easily persuaded that she is

'A lords sister' (II.iii.221) and scholar of divinity, now crazed in her wits. When Surly expresses some scepticism about the circumstances of this supposed lady, Sir Epicure at once protests that he knows her family well: her brother is 'one I honour, and my noble friend,/ And I respect his house' (II.iii.277–8). Having so swiftly persuaded himself of his familiarity with this house, Mammon has no difficulty in complying with Face's stipulation before his eventual meeting with the lady.

> Face   And you must praise her house, remember that,
>   And her nobilitie.
> Mammon   Let me, alone:
>   No *Herald*, no nor *Antiquarie*, *Lungs*,
>   Shall doe it better.   (IV.i.19–22)

Left alone with Dol, Mammon praises the 'strange nobilitie' of her eye, her lip, her chin.

>   Me thinkes you doe resemble
>   One of the *Austriack* princes.
> Face   Very like,
>   Her father was an *Irish* costar-monger.
> Mammon   The house of *Valois*, just, had such a nose.
>   And such a fore-head, yet the *Medici*
>   Of *Florence* boast.   (IV.i.54–60)

Such a lady, he believes, ought rightfully to live not in 'This nooke, here, of the *Friers*', but rather should 'come forth,/ And tast the aire of palaces' (IV.i.131, 134–5): her aristocratic house deserves a grander physical house to set off its dignities and beauties.

In preparing Mammon for this encounter, Face has warned him that he must make no mention of divinity to the lady, 'For feare of putting her in rage'.

> Mammon   I warrant thee.
> Face   Sixe men will not hold her downe. And then,
>   If the old man should heare, or see you—
> Mammon   Feare not.
> Face   The very house, sir, would runne mad.
>   (IV.i.10–13)

'*The very house*': Face is conjuring up another household to rival that of the supposedly aristocratic lady whom Mammon is about to

meet; this 'house' consists of Subtle, its apparent master, and his
mysterious retinue (none other than Face and Dol, in their many
guises). But Face's words also contain the further humorous
suggestion that the building which they now inhabit would itself be
affected by so grave a transgression as the mention of scriptural
controversy. In his meeting with Dol, Mammon contrives to break
not only Face's prohibition but also that of Subtle, who has told him
that if the elixir is to come to perfection, he must practise perfect
chastity, paying no regard to the opposite sex. Face has warned
Mammon that once the lady falls into her fit, she

> will discourse
> So learnedly of *genealogies*,
> As you would runne mad, too, to heare her, sir.   (II.iii.240–2)

And it is of genealogies—of the rise and fall of ancient families—that
Dol indeed discourses in her '*fit of talking*', prompted by Mammon's
indiscreet mention of his wish to establish a fifth monarchy.

> *Dol*   And so we may arrive by *Talmud* skill,
>   And profane *greeke*, to raise the building up
>   Of HELENS house, against the Ismaelite,
>   King of *Thogarma*, and his *Habergions*
>   Brimstony, blew, and fiery; and the force
>   Of King ABADDON, and the Beast of *Cittim*:
>   Which *Rabbi* DAVID KIMCHI, ONKELOS,
>   And ABEN-EZRA doe interpret *Rome*.   (IV.v.25–32)[16]

The pandemonium climaxes with the entrance of Subtle and '*A great
crack and noise within*'. It is indeed as though *the very house* has now run
mad, the edifice itself responding to Mammon's folly.

> *Subtle*   Hangs my roofe
> Over us still, and will not fall, o justice,
> Upon us, for this wicked man!   (IV.v.78–80)

Meanwhile, in another part of the house, Surly is at large,
disguised as a Spanish Count. Almost the first words which Surly
utters in this role concern the nature of the house:

[16] Dol's ravings are neatly lifted from the Puritan writer Hugh Broughton's *A Concent of Scripture* (1590); Dol quotes chiefly from Broughton's
commentary on Daniel's interpretation of Nebuchadnezzar's dream (Dan.
2), concerning the progressive degeneration of kingdoms.

Surly   *Por dios, Sennores, muy linda casa!*
Subtle   What sayes he?
Face   Praises the house, I thinke,
  I know no more but's action.
Subtle   Yes, the *Casa*,
  My precious DIEGO, will prove faire inough,
  To cossen you in. Doe you marke? you shall
  Be cossened, DIEGO.
Face   Cossened, doe you see?
  My worthy *Donzel*, cossened.
Surly   *Entiendo*.   (IV.iii.34–40)

'*Entiendo*', 'I understand'—as Surly indeed does understand, more
thoroughly than either Face or Subtle realizes. Surly professes to
praise the house *as a brothel*, which is indeed what he privately
believes it to be; it is an assignation that he is seemingly after, and he
pretends to a certain connoisseurship in the necessary arrangements
surrounding these matters. When Surly arrives, however, the only
available lady of the house, Dol Common, is busy with Sir Epicure,
and Face proposes to Subtle that they must persuade Dame Pliant to
stand in for Dol:

Face   What dost thou thinke on't, SUBTLE?
Subtle   Who, I? Why—
Face   The credit of our house too is engag'd.   (IV.iii.69–70)

'The credit of our house': Face makes their enterprise sound like that
of a firm of international bankers, and it is especially revealing that
the two of them should adopt such language in private conversation.
'Credit' means both credibility, the primary meaning of the word,
and financial solvency. For Face and Subtle, the two things are
closely connected, for people put their money where their beliefs
are, and it is thus upon belief that they constantly endeavour to play.
But how are Dame Pliant and her brother Kastril to be persuaded to
accept this substitution? The argument which convinces them both
is that of social advancement: the Spanish Count (they are told) is
keen to marry the widow, and, as Kastril contentedly remarks, 'This
match will advance the house of the KASTRILS' (IV.iv.88).
  'The house of the KASTRILS': the phrase confers upon an obscure
country family the pomp and status of a noble European dynasty.
The advancement of this house is to proceed more modestly than
Kastril anticipates. The aristocratic claims of the supposed Spanish

Count, like those of the supposed lady whom Mammon ardently
pursues, are to prove wholly fraudulent. The 'houses' to which these
characters seemingly belong exist merely in the imagination. So too
does the commercial house which Subtle and Face profess to operate,
and the house of retainers which Face pretends that Subtle has in his
employ. Both in the literal and the metaphorical senses of the phrase,
the three confidence workers have *no house* to support their
enterprises. In the opening scene of the play Face cuttingly reminds
Subtle that he is in fact a houseless person, a vagabond, and that it is
he, Face, who has provided him with the house in which he now
operates—a house, as Subtle is quick to respond, which does not
belong to Face, either.

> *Face*   I ga' you countenance, credit for your coales,
>   Your stills, your glasses, your *materialls*,
>   Built you a fornace, drew you customers,
>   Advanc'd all your black arts; lent you, beside,
>   A house to practise in—
> *Subtle*   Your masters house?
> *Face*   Where you have studied the more thriving skill
>   Of bawdrie, since.
> *Subtle*   Yes, in your masters house.   (I.i.43–9)

The alliance between Subtle, Face, and Dol is as temporary and
uncertain as their occupancy of Lovewit's premises; theirs is a *house*
in which little credit can be placed.

The various houses thus far described in *The Alchemist* are 'magic'
in the sense that they lack a basis in reality, existing principally in the
hopes and fantasies and perceptions of the characters themselves.
The almost empty house in Blackfriars is capable of becoming
whatever its occupants and visitors most wish it to become: closely
inspected after the event, it proves to be merely an almost empty
house in Blackfriars. Lovewit's house (in short) is irresistibly like
that other house—situated, in all probability, in Blackfriars too—
where this very play was first presented in 1610 by the King's Men.[17]
These two houses of illusion are in fact *the same house*, and the

---

[17] I follow F.H. Mares, editor of the Revels edition of *The Alchemist*
(London, 1967), p. lxv, in believing it more likely that the play was first
presented at Blackfriars than at the Globe, as Herford and Simpson assert.
For a fuller argument on this matter, see R.L. Smallwood's ' "Here, in the
Friars": Immediacy and Theatricality in *The Alchemist*', *RES*, n.s. 32 (1980),
pp. 142–60.

charlatans who arouse and exploit the fantasies of their victims are (when all is said and done) members of the company of the King's Men, who use similar arts to somewhat similar ends. For the playhouse is, par excellence, a magic house, a wooden frame animated and transformed by the skills of the actors, men who pretend to be what they are not, playing in a house that seems to be what it is not: closely inspected after the event, it is merely a wooden frame, an almost empty house in Blackfriars. 'Good faith, sir, I believe,/ There's no such thing', says Face to his master Lovewit in the last act of the play, coolly dismissing the confused gossip of the neighbours: ''Tis all *deceptio visus*' (V.iii.61–2). What has been glimpsed in and around Lovewit's house is simply an optical illusion, *deceptio visus*, lacking any basis in reality. And in a double sense, this might be regarded as true: for the confidence tricksters have indeed traded in deception, not substance, and (moreover) they themselves have been impersonated by a group of actors, whose business is likewise to deceive. Lovewit's house is thus a powerful analogue and symbol of the playhouse itself, with which it is in a sense coterminous. The charlatan's art is not unlike that of the dramatist and his actors, and there is thus a further uncomfortable resemblance between the audience who are currently enjoying this comedy and the gulls whom the charlatans are currently exploiting. Both groups of people have wandered expectantly into a house in Blackfriars where their fantasies are entertained; both groups have been gently relieved of their cash. *Caveat spectator*.

Though the warning note is there, it would be a mistake (I believe) to regard *The Alchemist* merely as a parable on the perils of theatre-going, or as a costive diatribe against 'the loathèd stage'. Jonson certainly exhibits from time to time what Jonas Barish has called the 'anti-theatrical prejudice',[18] but it is impossible to ignore the zest and high spirits of *The Alchemist*, the speed and delight with which the illusory arts are planned and executed. For the theatre, as the play reminds us, is a magic house in a pleasurable as well as a delusive sense, and the playwright's and actors' aim is not to drive their customers from the doors, but instead 'To feast you often, and invite new ghests' (V.v.165). The play is (so to speak) its own lode-stone, placed beneath the threshold to draw in visitors to the theatre. The

---

[18] Jonas A. Barish, 'Jonson and the Loathèd Stage', in *A Celebration of Ben Jonson*, ed. W. Blissett et al. (Toronto, 1974); and the same author's *The Antitheatrical Prejudice* (Berkeley, Los Angeles, London, 1981).

London theatres were in fact closed for substantial periods around
the time of the first performance of *The Alchemist*, on account of the
plague; if there was a risk of contagion in such public congregations
as the play now attracted, there must also now have been a particular
pleasure for actors and audience alike in seeing the playhouse open
and full of life.[19] The plague is an important background to the play
itself: it is on account of the plague that Lovewit has shut up his
London house and gone off to tend his hop-fields in the healthier air
of Kent. Like the authorities responsible for the closure of the
playhouses, Lovewit is watching the weekly mortality figures in
London in order to decide when to re-open his house.[20] When he
returns earlier than Face, Subtle, and Dol have calculated, Face
hastily concocts a story that the house has been infected by plague
during Lovewit's absence: the cat that kept the buttery had the
disease a week before Face noticed it, and so (Face continues) he
locked the house up prudently for a month,

> Purposing then, sir,
> T'have burnt rose-vinegar, triackle, and tarre,
> And, ha' made it sweet, that you should ne'er ha' knowne it.
> (V.ii.11–13)

Though the story is a fabrication, there is another, deeper, sense in
which Face—as Lovewit himself is soon to recognize—has
sweetened and revived his master's house. For this house has never
been, in the fullest sense, a *house* since the death of Lovewit's first
wife, as Subtle's contemptuous attack upon Face in the opening
scene of the play indirectly reveals.

> You, and the rats, here, kept possession.
> Make it not strange. I know, yo'were one, could keepe
> The buttry-hatch still lock'd, and save the chippings,
> Sell the dole-beere to *aqua-vitae*-men,
> The which, together with your *christ-masse* vailes,
> At *post and paire*, your letting out of counters,
> Made you a pretty stock, some twentie markes,
> And gave you credit, to converse with cob-webs,
> Here, since your mistris death hath broke up house.   (I.i.50–8)

[19] F.P. Wilson, *The Plague in Shakespeare's London* (Oxford, 1927), pp.
125–7.
[20] *The Alchemist*, I.i.182–3; IV.vii.115–18. On the effect of mortality rates
on the theatre closures, see Wilson, *The Plague in Shakespeare's London*, pp.
51–5.

Into this cobwebby house, 'broke up' and run down since the death
of his late mistress, Face brings new life and energy—and, for his
master, a new wife, Dame Pliant, who 'Will make you seven yeeres
yonger, and a rich one' (V.iii.86). This is not illusion: it is flesh and
blood, solid cash and solid 'happinesse' (V.v.147). A real magic has
been worked within the near-dead house, and a new and living one
established.

IV

The title page of Jonson's *Discoveries* carries a tag from Persius
(*Satires*, iv.52): *tecum habita, ut noris quam sit tibi curta supellex*—'live in
your own house, and recognize how poorly it is furnished'. Time
and again throughout his writing, Jonson praises those who live
soberly and stoically 'at home' within their own houses, recognizing
how poorly (or how sufficiently) they are furnished. Sir Robert
Wroth is praised as one who can avoid the temptations of the court
and city, and can 'at home, in thy securer rest,/ Live, with un-bought
provision blest' (*The Forest*, iii.13–14). The speaker of 'To the
World' vows to 'make my strengths, such as they are,/ Here in my
bosome, and at home' (*The Forest*, iv.67–8). John Selden has been
'Ever at home' though has 'all Countries seene' (*The Underwood*,
xiv.30). Sir Kenelm Digby is celebrated as an embodiment of virtue:
'And he is built like some imperiall roome/ For that to dwell in, and
be still at home' (*The Underwood*, lxxviii.7–8). To live 'at home' is to
recognize—undeceived, undeceivingly—one's own peculiar
strengths and limitations. Errant characters within Jonson's
comedies are often, as a final, chastening, punishment, *sent home*. In
Act Five, Scene Three of *Volpone* (for example) each of the legacy
hunters is curtly advised by Mosca to 'Go home'. 'Goe home, and
use the poore sir POL, your knight, well', he says to Lady Would-
be, 'For feare I tell some riddles' (44–5). To Corvino: 'Go home, be
melancholique too, or mad' (60). To Corbaccio: 'Go home, and die,
and stinke' (74). And to Voltore: 'Good faith, you looke / As you
were costive; best go home, and purge, sir' (100–1). In the following
scene, the great traveller Sir Politic Would-be, tormented by the
disguised Peregrine, clambers laboriously beneath a tortoise shell,
vowing 'to shunne, this place, and clime for ever; / Creeping, with
house, on backe' (87–8). The tortoise, which carried its own house
for ever on its back, was a familiar emblem of integrity, polity, and

self-containment: it remained for ever at home.[21] At the end of the play, the Avocatori send the innocent Celia 'Home, to her father, with her dowrie trebled' (V.xii.144): Celia, who has been so obsessively shut away by her husband Corvino in that other house in '*an obscure nooke of the* piazza' (II.ii.38) until the one catastrophic enforced venture to an apparently safe, apparently private house elsewhere, which has led to public exposure and humiliation.

The private house is thus for Jonson an important symbol of what Thomas M. Greene has called 'the centered self', that modest, gathered, stable, singular make of personality to which Jonson seemingly aspired.[22] As one ponders this symbol in relation to Jonson's own art and life, however, certain ironies are evident. 'Live in your own house, and recognize how poorly it is furnished' is (to begin with) a curious motto to affix to a commonplace book so densely furnished with transcriptions of the writings of other authors that a modern editor has argued 'that the *Discoveries* might be, without any serious objection, left out of the Jonsonian canon; that, practically, the book is not his; or, at least, that the merit and interest of it are for the most part attributable to other men'.[23] 'Live in your own house'? The arts of imitation, appropriation, and impersonation were clearly of absorbing interest to Jonson, both in literature and in life: imaginatively speaking, he lived in many other 'houses', just as—in the most literal sense—he chose for many years to leave his own house and live contentedly in the homes of various friends and patrons.[24] Though Jonson vowed on more than one occasion to leave 'the loathèd stage', it was in that magical house—delusive and unstable in its presentations and its rewards—that he was paradoxically most at home.

Within the world of his comedies, a part at least of Jonson's complex sympathies is reserved for the shifty and the shiftless, the men and women who live by their wits, not their estates, who have neither a fixed identity nor a fixed home. To hide oneself away from

[21] Ian Donaldson, 'Jonson's Tortoise', *RES*, n.s. 19 (1968), pp. 162–6.
[22] Thomas M. Greene, 'Ben Jonson and the Centered Self', *SEL 1500–1900*, 10 (1970), pp. 325–48.
[23] Ben Jonson, *Discoveries*, ed. Maurice Castelain (Paris and London, n.d. [1906]), p. vii.
[24] In 1602, according to Manningham's diary, Jonson was living with Sir Robert Townshend; later he lived for five years with Esmé Stewart, Lord Aubigny; in 1603 he was staying, probably briefly, with Sir Robert Cotton at Conington in Huntingdonshire.

the world in a fortified and sound-proofed house, as Morose in *The Silent Woman* attempts forlornly to do, is—as that comedy shows—to prize that 'centered self' more highly than the freedom and openness which make a person truly human. It may be a fit punishment for Sir Politic Would-be that he is forced finally to creep within the shell of a tortoise, who moves for ever with his house upon his back, but that creature is scarcely a satisfactory model for human emulation. The fox, that devious and lively sallier-out from home, seems altogether more engaging in its ways.

It is one of the ironies of Jonson's own life that during his final years, crippled by strokes and palsy, he was confined to a single room of his house in Westminster, now at last constantly 'at home', as house-bound and bed-bound as his own dramatic character Volpone had once feigned to be. Grossly overweight, he lay (his muse, he complained, as restricted as he)

> ... block'd up, and straightned, narrow'd in,
> Fix'd to the bed, and boords, unlike to win
> Health, or scarce breath ...   (*The Underwood*, lxxi. 10–12)

The single room that had been so favourite a theme and setting in his plays was now his own daily and unvarying experience. In 1631 a friend possessed of a touching thoughtfulness and humour presented the invalid with a pet fox: 'wch Creature', wrote Jonson, 'by handling, I endeavoured to make tame, aswell for the abateing of my disease, as the delight I tooke in speculation of his Nature'.[25] And what did the fox think about his own enforced confinement to an urban house? As it happens, an answer of sorts is to hand. Writing to the Earl of Newcastle shortly before Christmas 1631, Jonson reports a dream that he has recently had. A servant arrives at his bedside and announces, 'Master, Master the Foxe speakes'.

> Whereat, (mee thought) I started, and troubled, went downe into the Yard, to witnes the wonder; There I found my Reynard, in his Tenement the Tubb, I had hyr'd for him, cynically expressing his owne lott, to be condemn'd to the house of a Poett, where nothing was to bee seene but the bare walls, and not any thing heard but the noise of a Sawe, dividing billatts all the weeke long, more to keepe the family in exercise, then to comfort any person

---

[25] This and the following quotations are from Jonson's letter to the Earl of Newcastle, 20 December 1630, in Herford and Simpson, I.213–14.

there with fire, save the Paralytick master; and went on in this
way as the Foxe seem'd the better Fabler, of the two.

The fox informs his master that the cellar is infested with moles. The
royal mole-catcher is fetched, but announces that there is nothing he
can do; only the king or some nobleman can remedy the situation.

This kind of Mole is call'd a *Want*, wch will distroy you, and your
family, if you prevent not the workeing of it in tyme, And
therefore, god keepe you and send you health.

A 'want' is a species of mole, and Jonson's house—as he wittily and
beseechingly reports to Newcastle—is undermined by a *want*: is
there nothing that his lordship can do at this Christmas time to
relieve it?[26] The imagination that had once been stirred (if Aubrey is
to be credited) by the thought of Thomas Sutton's confinement to a
house which threatened to collapse through the weight of chests of
money now is exercised by a meditation on his own confinement,
and by the fantasy of the collapse of his own house through 'want'.
In his greatest comedy, a man behaves like a fox; in this dream of his
old age, a fox behaves like a man, frankly discussing with its master
the miseries of confined living, and the perils that threaten their
house. The constrained and the free, the centred and the eccentric,
the housed and the houseless, the fast and the loose, remained to the
end of Ben Jonson's life the great polarities between which his
creative imagination moved.

[26] Cf. the play in Jonson's 'Epistle Mendicant' to Lord Weston, the Lord
High Treasurer, in the same year: '*Disease*, the Enemie, and his Ingineeres,/
Want, with the rest of his conceal'd compeeres,/ Have cast a trench about
mee, now, five yeares': *The Underwood*, lxxi.4–6.

IV

Samuel Johnson's Literary Criticism

JOHN HARDY

Long ago I wrote of Johnson as a literary critic that 'the personally realized quality of his dialectic ... differentiates him from other critics within seemingly the same critical tradition'.[1] I have found no reason to change this view. Johnson's is still criticism we turn to when we wish to know what an acutely sensitive and intelligent mind has said about the works of Shakespeare or Milton or Dryden or Pope. We resort to literary criticism when, as readers of literature ourselves, we want to be stimulated or challenged; and Johnson's criticism has stood the test of time by remaining both stimulating and challenging. While we may sometimes disagree with particular judgements, his full-bodied assessments of works or authors argue his peculiarly human, complex responsiveness to great works of the imagination in both poetry and drama.

Historians of criticism have so often lumped Johnson together with his neo-classical contemporaries that one has to insist his own criticism is distinctive from (as well as more distinguished than) theirs. Even Dryden, whom Johnson called 'the father of English criticism',[2] tended to write with an eye on the object or end-product of his own poetic workshop. What he says is in general oriented towards the work of art as such rather than the kind of response an audience might have to it. The pervasive orientation of Johnson's criticism is, however, different, and may be glimpsed in his unforgettable note on Falstaff ('Falstaff unimitated, unimitable Falstaff, how shall I describe thee?'), or that vivid reminder we are given in the Preface of Johnson himself as a member of Shakespeare's audience: 'As he commands us, we laugh or mourn, or sit silent with quiet expectation, in tranquillity without indifference.'[3]

[1] 'Two Notes on Johnson', *Johnsonian Studies*, ed. Magdi Wahba (Cairo, 1962), p. 226.

[2] *Johnson's Lives of the Poets: A Selection*, ed. J.P. Hardy (Clarendon Press, Oxford, 1971), p. 160. All subsequent quotations from the *Lives* are taken from this edition.

[3] Quotations from Johnson's Shakespearian criticism are taken from *Johnson on Shakespeare*, ed. Arthur Sherbo, Yale Edition of the Works of Samuel Johnson, vols. VII–VIII (New Haven and London, 1968): VII.523, 68.

Johnson's distinctiveness can also be suggested by comparing his remarks on *King Lear* with the kind of position that Dennis's criticism, say, implies. Dennis supported the notion of 'poetical justice' by making Rymer's point even more emphatically: for him the justice which the poet meted out to his 'creatures' was a 'type' (however imperfect) of the Judgement of the divine Creator towards His—so that, unless in drama the good were rewarded and the wicked punished, Providence would appear but as Chance or Fate.[4] Something of this same concern was arguably part of Johnson's reaction as well, but the difference between them as literary critics becomes obvious when we set Johnson's comments on *Lear* against Dennis's more general discussion of the question. Dennis in fact shows no awareness of *Lear* as a play needing special discussion; indeed, his easy optimism (moral complacency even) in considering the general question is no part of Johnson's own response. Whatever the various resonances that enter into this response, Johnson gives voice (as Dennis is unable to) to what we feel adds to the pain of this play's ending: 'All reasonable beings naturally love justice' (VIII.704). *King Lear* defeats our expectation of justice, carrying us to the very edge of the stark and searing. What is felt at the end involves that from which Johnson instinctively recoiled, namely, that life itself provides no answer to Lear's final question—no answer, except that life is as it is and must be faced as such.

It will be clear, then, that Johnson's criticism is more than historically interesting. Indeed, it is both of an age and for all time. While the tradition which he inherited imparted an unmistakable flavour to his critical pronouncements, what needs to be stressed is the often creative use he made of it—the positive way in which it influenced but for the most part did not shackle his critical thinking. There are, of course, those few pronouncements which now seem quaint or wrong-headed, like the notorious condemnation of Milton's *Lycidas*; but for the most part the tradition within which Johnson wrote provided a kind of informing principle to the serious activity of mind he brought to the discussion of literature. What we have to consider is both the tradition and the man since Johnson's activity of mind is obviously shaped by his own personal attitudes and predispositions. And the tensions that can arise as a result of this

---

[4] *The Critical Works of John Dennis*, ed. E.N. Hooker (Baltimore, 1939–43), II.6, 20–1.

level of imaginative commitment inevitably contribute to the personally realized quality of Johnson's dialectic.

Sometimes these tensions, or even inconsistencies, stem from contradictory assumptions. For example, Johnson assumes, with Aristotle, that the excellence of art is the excellence of truth—'just representations of general nature'. Yet he was so 'perpetually' a moralist as also to assume that 'it is always a writer's duty to make the world better'.[5] The question therefore arises, to what extent must nature be edited or left unedited? Or, to put this in other words, can Johnson praise Shakespeare for exhibiting 'the real state of sublunary nature' and also criticize him for failing to compromise the way nature actually is?

Johnson ends his general note on *As You Like It* with this sentence:

> By hastening to the end of his work Shakespeare suppressed the dialogue between the usurper and the hermit, and lost an opportunity of exhibiting a moral lesson in which he might have found matter worthy of his highest powers.   (VII.265)

Again, when Juliet says to the Nurse, 'Leave me to myself to-night;/ For I have need of many orisons', Johnson's gratuitous comment brings a smile to our lips: 'Juliet plays most of her pranks under the appearance of religion; perhaps Shakespeare meant to punish her hypocrisy' (VIII.953). Yet Johnson's imaginative and moral engagement with Shakespeare's world is also his strength as a critic, and a good example is his analysis of King John's reproach of Hubert on being told that the boy Arthur has been murdered:

> A man engaged in wickedness would keep the profit to himself, and transfer the guilt to his accomplice. These reproaches vented against Hubert are not the words of art or policy, but the eruptions of a mind swelling with consciousness of a crime, and desirous of discharging its misery on another.   (VII.425)

This note (of which I have quoted only part) gives a glimpse into the heart of the action. Johnson's characteristic concern with morals and motives is here sharpened to a fine relevance as he penetrates the facade of 'That smooth-faced gentleman, tickling Commodity' so much in evidence throughout this play.

The inherent tensions that can exist in and through Johnson's

---

[5] See *Johnson's Lives*, p. 59; *Johnson on Shakespeare*, VII.71.

imaginative and moral engagement with Shakespeare's world are there (co-existing, so to speak) in his note on *King Lear*. Whatever his reservations about Shakespeare's tragic ending, he significantly begins his note on the play with these words:

> The tragedy of Lear is deservedly celebrated among the dramas of Shakespeare. There is perhaps no play which keeps the attention so strongly fixed; which so much agitates our passions and interests our curiosity . . . So powerful is the current of the poet's imagination, that the mind, which once ventures within it, is hurried irresistibly along.   (VIII.702–3)

Once again we see Johnson as a member of Shakespeare's audience responding to what is before him. Such a passage gives weight to his implicit claim in the Preface that it was Shakespeare's ability to 'instruct by pleasing' (VII.67)—a formulation that significantly moves beyond the usual Horatian tag of *prodesse aut delectare* by integrating what had often been regarded as potentially diverse elements within a single process. However Shakespeare might have *seemed* to Johnson 'to write without any moral purpose' (VII.71), the whole burden of the Preface testifies to Shakespeare's human centrality, his 'human sentiments in human language' (VII.65), and hence our vivid interest in and engagement with his scenes. By holding the 'mirrour' up to nature, Shakespeare provides Johnson with the means of looking intimately at human life. Indeed, what Johnson takes to be instructive about good biography can be applied, *mutatis mutandis*, to his appreciation of Shakespeare's characters. By being moved to experience the plays, a member of Shakespeare's audience would be able to glimpse human nature at first-hand and therefore learn something important. As Johnson himself says, in commenting on the lifelikeness of Shakespeare's characterization: 'It is from this wide extension of design that so much instruction is derived' (p. 62).

Johnson's terminology in adumbrating Shakespeare's achieve-ment has, nevertheless, often been misunderstood. 'In the writings of other poets', he says, 'a character is too often an individual; in those of Shakespeare it is commonly a species' (VII.62). By 'indi-vidual' Johnson did not mean what we mean by an individualized character. He was, after all, the critic who, objecting to the 'nar-rower principles' of a Rymer, Dennis, or Voltaire, defended Shakespeare for presenting on stage a foolish senator or a drunken

king. Shakespeare's 'persons', he says, 'act and speak by the influence of those general passions and principles by which all minds are
agitated, and the whole system of life is continued in motion'
(VII.62). It is as though the dramatist has had them drink from that
phial which Henry Fielding described as 'the pathetic potion'—'a
mixture of all the passions, but in no exact proportion', so that from
every mixture or combination a different character is formed.[6] Johnson himself viewed the Shakespearian character as possessing a
broad range of human traits as well as a distinctive individuality.
And in taking his stand on 'nature', he saw more clearly than his
contemporaries what makes Shakespeare a classic. What so substantiates his plays to the imagination is his ability to provide a
context for the actions of his characters, as though working in an
inward and non-reductive way from various human centres.
Shakespeare's representation of human nature is, then, conceived
and ordered in a particular way—dramatically, imaginatively, and
yet at the same time objectively and impersonally. This is clearly an
achievement which might be described as classical, involving as it
does a peculiarly apt and dramatic tempering of human experience.

When Walter Raleigh's *Johnson on Shakespeare* first appeared, a
reviewer suggested that it might appropriately have its title turned
around. For a personality and literary intelligence as large as Johnson's, contact with Shakespeare is inevitably revealing of the critic
as well as the writer. A tantalizing example of this is afforded by
Johnson's criticism of *Macbeth*—a play which interested him from an
early period since he used it in 1745 to provide a sample of his skills as
an aspiring editor of Shakespeare. Parts, at least, of the play had for
him an extraordinary immediacy, since in his comparison of the
respective descriptions of night by Shakespeare and Dryden, Johnson comments: 'He that peruses Shakespeare, looks round alarmed,
and starts to find himself alone' (VIII.770). Yet this kind of interest
or immediacy is apparently not borne out by Johnson's general note
on the play; indeed, the more we look at what he says there, the more
curious it becomes. Are there grounds for suggesting that the note is
something of a rationalization, as though its real message must be
read between the lines—as though the play somehow troubled
Johnson more than his apparently confident summary of it would
seem to allow?

Johnson's note on *Macbeth* is as follows:

---

[6] *A Journey from This World to the Next*, chapter 6.

This play is deservedly celebrated for the propriety of its fictions, and solemnity, grandeur, and variety of its action; but it has no nice discriminations of character, the events are too great to admit the influence of particular dispositions, and the course of the action necessarily determines the conduct of the agents.

The danger of ambition is well described; and I know not whether it may not be said in defence of some parts which now seem improbable, that, in Shakespeare's time, it was necessary to warn credulity against vain and illusive predictions.

The passions are directed to their true end. Lady Macbeth is merely detested; and though the courage of Macbeth preserves some esteem, yet every reader rejoices at his fall.   (VIII.795)

It seems curious that Johnson should praise the 'action' of the play and yet find fault with 'the course of the action' on the grounds that the main characters (and especially Macbeth) are entangled in something too big for them, as though robbed of effective moral choice and therefore not answerable for their actions. If the implications of what Johnson is saying are these, then how can every reader be in a position to 'rejoice' at Macbeth's fall? The question nevertheless remains why Johnson approached the play in these terms, and assumed that 'the course of the action' was indeed so overpowering as to make Macbeth a virtual puppet.

The action of *Macbeth* is, of course, singularly economical: the future is caught in the instant; what is prophesied comes, almost ineluctably, to pass. While Johnson's note registers a sense of this, the 1773 edition of Johnson and George Steevens included an earlier note suggesting that the 'weird sisters' are to be seen as the three goddesses of destiny. Moreover, from the time of his earlier *Miscellaneous Observations* Johnson had proposed that the lines, 'Which fate, and metaphysical aid, doth seem / To have thee crown'd withal', should be amended: 'For "seem" the sense evidently directs us to read "seek". The crown to which fate destines thee, and which preternatural agents "endeavour" to bestow upon thee' (VII.15). To what extent, then, was Johnson seeking to read this play in the very terms in which he criticized or condemned it?

Though it may be argued that in this play Shakespeare raises the question of the identity and autonomy of the individual self, Johnson was always so insistent in maintaining the freedom of the will that in the almost unconscious inner convolutions of his note he was perhaps seeking to sidestep this issue by assuming that Macbeth was predestined to act as he does—thereby removing his actions from the sphere of moral responsibility and scrutiny. Certainly Johnson does not attribute to Macbeth the kind of awareness or introspection which makes him for us such a tragic figure. In his note on the speech where Macbeth reports his sight of the murdered Duncan, Johnson comments as follows:

> It is not improbable, that Shakespeare put these forced and un-natural metaphors into the mouth of Macbeth as a mark of artifice and dissimulation, to show the difference between the studied language of hypocrisy, and the natural outcries of sudden passion.
> (VIII.774)

Clearly there is here a contrast with the way in which we would regard the speech—as an almost involuntary or unconscious ack-nowledgement of the enormity of 'Ruin's wasteful entrance' by a Macbeth not yet 'in blood / Stept in so far' that he can remain entirely unmoved by what he sees before him.

The next paragraph of Johnson's note also seems to contain an element of rationalization: 'I know not whether it may not be said in defence of some parts which now seem improbable, that, in Shakespeare's time, it was necessary to warn credulity against vain and illusive predictions.' This invoking, as it were, of the concept of an historical imagination certainly gels with Johnson's opening note on the play. There he states:

> A poet who should now make the whole action of his tragedy depend upon enchantment, and produce the chief events by the assistance of supernatural agents, would be censured as transgres-sing the bounds of probability, be banished from the theatre to the nursery, and condemned to write fairy tales instead of tragedies.
> (VIII.752)

Yet *Macbeth* is by no means a fairy tale, even though it contains an element of the fantastic that can be dressed up in a rather operatic way. Again it could be said that in this long opening note Johnson is protesting too much, is once again seeking grounds to push the play further from him. It is as though an impeccable rationalism is per-suading itself to ignore the claims of close analysis. While this must remain a suggestion on this side of certainty, Johnson's note clearly has a tone of some discomfiture about it.

The third paragraph of Johnson's general note seems to provide further confirmation that in his written statement he has shied away from a central question the play raises. Admittedly it is possible to see a degree of truth in what Johnson is saying. Yet the fifth act is not an insignificant part of the play since it pulls together and plays on those strands which a more Machiavellian interpretation of the central characters chooses to ignore. Lady Macbeth is surely not 'merely detested' after the sleep-walking scene; nor is it only 'the courage' of Macbeth in the fifth act which 'preserves some esteem'. Shakespeare is there concerned to engage our feelings for Macbeth on many levels of attention, so that it is not just his bravado in the face of seemingly overwhelming odds which 'preserves some esteem'. Besides his apparent concern for his wife—'She should have died hereafter;/ There would have been a time for such a word'—there is, above all, his poignant realization of what it must be like to live under the kind of tyrant he has become. He must expect 'Curses (not loud, but deep), mouth-honour, breath/ Which the poor heart would fain deny and dare not.' It is not, then, just 'the courage' of Macbeth at bay that makes his tragedy convincing, and for this reason it is inappropriate to conclude that 'every reader *rejoices* at his fall'—as though the audience, however involved in the final action, is no more ambivalent than the avenging Malcolm or Macduff. My suggestion is that Johnson found it convenient to be so unambivalent, easily adopting the righteous view while at the same time (not very consistently) maintaining that we are in no position to judge Macbeth because 'the course of the action necessarily determines the conduct of the agents'. Is Johnson having it both ways? And is he prompted to do so—to see the play as, in a sense, so cut-and-dried—because this enables him to distance himself from what he might otherwise have found disturbing?

What I have been implying about Johnson's criticism of *Macbeth* is not, of course, a stricture in any outright sense. Rather it is a mark of his strength as a critic that his engagement with literature is so real. Even seeming inconsistencies or self-contradictions can, for that very reason, be instructive, for in Johnson's sometimes divided response, in the capacity his mind has to be embattled against itself, we can be alerted to see more deeply into a work. His criticism of *Paradise Lost* is a case in point, despite the attempt that has been made to denature its degree of involvement by regarding it as merely a demonstration of some general critical method. What we have is not the dispassionate recital of the evidence on both sides, with the critic acting out the role of 'moderator, considering both sides of the argument to reach his judgment',[7] for it is only by being aware of Johnson himself *in* the criticism (rather than as somehow outside or independent of it) that we can begin to see it in all its fascinating complexity.

Though Johnson was committed for moral and religious reasons to the epic's grand 'design', another side of his nature or temperament was compelled to acknowledge the poem's 'want of human interest'—and as he argues out this point with himself, it clearly functions as something more than a mere 'inconvenience' of the poem's 'design' (*Lives*, pp. 105–7). *Paradise Lost* moved Johnson in some ways inexorably, but not, apparently, in others.

The ways in which it moved him can be readily cited. Because Johnson wrote of heaven and the fallen angels in the present tense, Milton's subject was for him not myth but sacred history. And because it was therefore founded on fixed and immutable truth—a truth, moreover, that had inescapable consequences for every human creature—it received Johnson's unqualified assent. His imagination was also excited by the 'sublimity' of its presentation: Milton brought to his subject 'an imagination in the highest degree fervid and active'—'the power of displaying the vast, illuminating the splendid, enforcing the awful, darkening the gloomy, and aggravating the dreadful' (p. 103). Yet, as this last phrase suggests, the irony was that *Paradise Lost* impinged so nearly and so painfully on Johnson's sensibility that he could not contemplate it with equanimity:

> Poetical pleasure must be such as human imagination can at least conceive, and poetical terror such as human strength and fortitude may combat. The good and evil of eternity are too ponderous for the wings of wit; the mind sinks under them in passive helplessness, content with calm belief and humble adoration.   (p. 106)

Following the psychological explanation of the 'sublime' posited by his friend Edmund Burke, Johnson accepted that whatever was 'terrible' should be far enough removed to seem also pleasurable—that a certain distance was necessary to ensure the aesthetic appreciation of an intense emotional effect. Yet Johnson was often unable to remove himself the necessary distance from the emotional intensity of *Paradise Lost*, for, despite what he says of 'calm belief and humble

[7] D.M. Hill, 'Johnson as Moderator', *N&Q*, 201 (1956), p. 522.

adoration', the poem's 'awful scenes' tended to remain for him 'simply terrible'.[8]

This represents what I should call the tortured side of Johnson's sensibility—what Boswell referred to as those 'wild beasts of the *Arena*' ready to spring from their dens in his remarkably suggestive comparison of Johnson's mind with the vast amphitheatre of the Roman Colosseum.[9] Another side of Johnson, however, found *Paradise Lost* lacking in human interest; and it is indicative of the constant challenge of his criticism that this criticism of Milton's great poem has remained hard to answer. In the words of A. J. A. Waldock,

> The conflict in our response to *Paradise Lost* is far from nominal ... The poem ... requires us ... with the full weight of our minds to believe that Adam did right, and simultaneously requires us with the full weight of our minds to believe that he did wrong.[10]

Waldock was, of course, referring to that unforgettable moment in Book IX when Adam chooses to fall with Eve; yet one has no means of knowing whether Johnson had this episode in mind when he said of the poem that 'the passions are moved only on one occasion'. He could have been referring to a passage in the early part of the poem; or he could have been referring to a passage from Book X. Perhaps he found it difficult to approach too closely the passage in Book IX; and yet one cannot help thinking that if he had been able to comment in detail upon it, he would have come even closer to the central problem the poem raises. Had he been able to do this, he would inevitably have sharpened the dilemma his criticism of *Paradise Lost* suggests, namely, his necessity to be a passionate and involved believer in its stated doctrine at the same time as he proves himself to be a confirmed and passionate humanist. Here especially we sense that his mind was embattled against itself.

While it has often been suggested that Johnson was most at home with poetry written in the Augustan mode, this view can obviously be pushed too far. Admittedly Boswell once heard him say: 'Sir, a thousand years may elapse before there shall appear another man with a power of versification equal to that of Pope.'[11] Yet Johnson's

[8] *A Philosophical Enquiry into the Origin of our Ideas of the Sublime and Beautiful* (London, 1759, 2nd edn, corr.), p. 60.

[9] See *Boswell's Life of Johnson*, ed. G.B. Hill, rev. L.F. Powell (Clarendon Press, Oxford, 1934–50), II.106.

[10] *Paradise Lost and its Critics* (Cambridge, 1947), p. 56.

[11] *Life of Johnson*, IV.46.

appraisal of Pope arguably leaves (as I shall later suggest) something to be desired. Moreover, one of the impressive things about Johnson's criticism is that, with very few exceptions, he responds to genuine poetic originality in whatever form, even when it seemingly challenges inherited preconceptions. 'Dr Johnson's spectacles' are, then, less inhibiting to him as a critic of poetry than has sometimes been assumed.[12] Rather one could say that Johnson's perceptions were robust enough to enable him to see around the limitations of his own preconceptions; and in this sense his criticism has a healthy open-endedness, being far removed (for all its remarkable authoritativeness) from the narrowly doctrinaire.

Consider, for example, his celebrated criticism of the metaphysical poets. Like his critical forbears and contemporaries, Johnson regards elegiac poetry written in this mode as a nonsense. Applied to such poetry, the term 'metaphysical' becomes one of dispraise—a boo rather than a clap. To this extent Johnson's criticism of the metaphysical mode is a blanket one, and as such too little responsive to what must be the basis for distinguishing between the good and the less good, namely, a discriminating analysis of the experience presented by or in a given poem. Yet even as Johnson states his view there are indications that he shrewdly discerns something positive as well. Of the celebrated compass image in Donne's *A Valediction: forbidding Mourning*, he says: 'It may be doubted whether absurdity or ingenuity has the better claim' (p. 26). This may not seem much like praise; yet we should remember that 'ingenuity' was probably a stronger word for Johnson than it sometimes is today. There is, too, Johnson's positive response to what he saw as the metaphysical poets' main achievement:

> If they frequently threw away their wit upon false conceits, they likewise sometimes struck out unexpected truth; if their conceits were far-fetched, they were often worth the carriage . . . No man could be born a metaphysical poet, nor assume the dignity of a writer, by descriptions copied from descriptions, by imitations borrowed from imitations, by traditional imagery and hereditary similes, by readiness of rhyme and volubility of syllables.
>
> (p. 13)

Such a passage deservedly throws a long shadow on much of the undistinguished verse of the Augustan period.

[12] See M.H. Abrams, 'Dr. Johnson's Spectacles', in *New Light on Dr. Johnson*, ed. F.W. Hilles (New Haven, 1959), pp. 177ff.

Johnson's criticism of the metaphysical poets inevitably raises his whole attitude to diction in poetry. Indeed, he remarks in the *Life of Cowley*: 'The diction, being the vehicle of the thoughts, first presents itself to the intellectual eye, and if the first appearance offends a further knowledge is not often sought' (p. 45). One cannot be too dogmatic about where precisely Johnson stood on this whole question. Pre-Saussure, certainly, for he belonged to a tradition and to an age which thought rather dichotomously about thought and expression (or 'sentiments' and 'diction'), as though trying to establish some connection between 'words' and 'things'. Yet despite a number of statements suggesting that poetic diction involved for Johnson an intrinsically selective vocabulary, one notices also the stress he seems to have placed on context, on (as he puts it in the *Life of Dryden*) 'those happy *combinations* of words which distinguish poetry from prose' (pp. 166–7—my italics).

Because of the assumptions about language which Johnson shared with his age, we are forced to question his ability to appreciate that realizing power of language which so singularly substantiates Shakespeare's work to the imagination. Nevertheless, on those rare occasions in the *Lives* where Johnson makes at least a gesture towards a more 'practical' criticism, he can certainly demonstrate his alertness to the realizing power of a particular passage of poetry. In praising the 'energy' of Dryden's verse, he seems to mean by this the whole creative vigour of the poet as this is displayed in his 'strength of expression' (one of Johnson's definitions of *energy* in the *Dictionary*). One passage he singles out for praise is the description of Shaftesbury in *The Medal*. The opening lines of this portrait are especially vivid:

> Power was his aim: but, thrown from that pretence,
> The wretch turned loyal in his own defence,
> And malice reconciled him to his prince.

Here the 'happy combinations' of language ('wretch turned loyal', 'malice reconciled') may be taken to suggest how internally disruptive was Shaftesbury's political schizophrenia.

In comparing Dryden and Pope, Johnson defined poetic 'genius', 'that power which constitutes a poet', as 'that energy which collects, combines, amplifies and animates' (p. 285). While such a passage does not wholly invalidate F.R. Leavis's point that Johnson was unable to appreciate the 'exploratory-creative' use of language that is characteristically associated with Shakespeare,[13] it does nevertheless suggest the importance he attached to the realizing power of the poetic imagination in its use of language. His response was therefore more flexible than has sometimes been supposed; and if further evidence were needed, one might point to the linguistic density and creativity that his own best poetry exhibits. William Empson cites examples from *The Vanity of Human Wishes* to illustrate his argument in *Seven Types of Ambiguity*; and he could have chosen better examples, like the opening lines of the portrait of Wolsey, or certain lines in the portrait of Charles of Sweden.

Though Johnson finds in Dryden's poetry 'brighter paragraphs' than in Pope's, he judges Pope's to be 'better poems' (p. 285). Among those he rates highest is *The Rape of the Lock*, and important here are the terms in which he praises it—the way in which it realizes its subject: 'In this work are exhibited in a very high degree the two most engaging powers of an author. New things are made familiar, and familiar things are made new' (p. 291). Johnson here talks of the *two* most engaging powers of an author, but he seems above all to recognize the important sense in which Pope is a poet or 'maker': 'New things are *made* familiar, and familiar things are *made* new.' Whereas Joseph Warton had criticized Pope for not writing like a Milton, Johnson's perception of what is important in poetry allows him to interpret imagination in a more flexible and relevant way. This allows him to approach different poets with a more inclusive sensibility and a more discriminating critical intelligence.

We need, however, to make different assessments of the critical sections of the two major *Lives* of Dryden and of Pope, and that we need to do so suggests some qualification to the general view that Johnson was most at home in dealing with those poets who wrote within the Augustan tradition. For a variety of reasons, the *Life of Dryden* is something of a masterpiece; in this sense it adequately justifies the ambition its author had so long entertained to write this poet's life. It conveys a sense of the emergence of Dryden as a figure of real importance, not merely through his Augustan-ness, but through the development of his origins in earlier seventeenth-century poetry. Moreover, Johnson does not only delineate Dryden's strengths; he also has a perceptive sense of certain limitations. Dryden's witty detachment in describing the Great Fire of London in *Annus Mirabilis* is condemned as a failure of sensibility,

[13] *The Common Pursuit* (London, 1953), p. 109.

as an inability to feel that distress at human suffering which Johnson himself can so vividly imagine. 'Dryden's was not', says Johnson, 'one of the "gentle bosoms" ' (a quotation from *Tyrannic Love*); 'He is . . . with all his variety of excellence not often pathetic' (p. 193). Johnson was perhaps thinking primarily of the plays, but his remark can also be applied to much of the poetry. Finding there little evidence of the mind that suffers or the heart that feels, Johnson was forced to conclude: 'He could more easily fill the ear with some splendid novelty than awaken those ideas that slumber in the heart' (p. 193). This remark is not, of course, true of Dryden's lines on Oldham or of his epistle to Congreve, but these were poems that Johnson might not have had in front of him when he wrote.

The critical section of the *Life of Pope* is, by comparison, curiously unsatisfactory. Admittedly, Johnson conveys his positive delight at Pope's incredibly rich and fertile imagery, as well as his very real sense of the poet's being a consummate master of his craft. Yet, despite this, a sense of dissatisfaction persists, and can, perhaps, be registered in terms of challenges which, for one reason or another, Johnson fails properly to take up. By these I mean not just Warton's challenging of Pope's reputation as a poet, but the challenge which for Johnson a poem like *The Dunciad* implicitly contained.

Warton's proposed method for testing whether a passage of poetry was 'pure' was 'to drop entirely the measures and numbers, and transpose and invert the order of words' and read it as prose. 'If', he continued, 'there be really in it a true poetical spirit, all your inversions and transpositions will not disguise and extinguish it.'[14] In neither his review of Warton nor his *Life of Pope* did Johnson directly challenge this assumption. Instead it was the relatively minor and odd figure (and neighbour of his) Percival Stockdale who argued that a poet's work could properly be approached only on its own terms. Part of Stockdale's answer to Warton is worth quoting here because it assumes the kind of analysis which 'practical criticism' aims at, but which appears all too infrequently throughout Johnson's *Lives*:

A particle may be so placed in a verse, that the sense of the Authour may be clear, and the idiom of our language may not be violated; yet even that particle, by a happy transposition, might

[14] *An Essay on the Genius and Writings of Pope* (London, 1762, 2nd edn, corr.), pp. vii–viii.

acquire life, and energy, and give more animation, and lustre to
the line. In the production of the fine arts, nothing is indifferent;
the minutest parts have their great importance and influence; they
reflect proportion, and expression on the other parts, from which
they likewise draw those advantages; and all the parts, as they are
disposed, and compacted by the artist, form a striking whole.[15]

Unfortunately much of Stockdale's later work does not show this
kind of lucidity; nevertheless had Johnson taken this invitation to
descend to particulars, he might well have illuminated Pope's poetry
by genuinely answering Warton, instead of relying on a somewhat
rhetorical display of putting him down.

Because of the dearth of close analysis (except in the earlier review
of Pope's epitaphs), we have a sharper sense of the inadequacy of
some of the comments on individual poems. For example, though
Johnson praises *Windsor-Forest* for its 'art of interchanging
description, narrative and morality' (p. 286), he shows little or no
sense of the tensions latent in it, or the means by which Pope
attempts their resolution. Again, the least convincing part of *An
Epistle to Dr Arbuthnot*—'the poet's vindication of his own
character'—is said to be the best, while the Sporus passage is
dismissed without further comment as 'the meanest' in the poem (p.
299). Yet most delimiting are Johnson's comments on *The Dunciad*.
While he notes that it 'affords perhaps the best specimen that has yet
appeared of personal satire ludicrously pompous' (p. 296), it is such a
reading of the poem as suggests the limits of Johnson's appraisal.

Johnson was disinclined to believe the author's claim that 'the
design was moral', even though he allowed the culpability of dulness
when it pretended to something else. Above all, however, Johnson
felt such disgust at 'the grossness' of many of the poem's images that
he was unable to view these as part of a serious poetic purpose, as
integral to the poem's incredible energy and imaginative vision.
While it is difficult to talk about such things in summary terms, they
are to be discerned in the local exuberance of Pope's verse—and
particularly, perhaps, in the portrait of the 'dauntless infant' of Book
IV. Johnson did include this passage among the poem's best, but
virtually gave no reason for doing so. Our attempt to do so would
involve drawing out its particular significance and, beyond this,
relating it to the poem as a whole. The destination of the 'dauntless

---

[15] *An Inquiry into the Nature and Genuine Laws of Poetry, including a particular
Defence of the Writings and Genius of Mr. Pope* (London, 1778), pp. 7–8.

infant' on his Grand Tour is that city where 'naked Venus' keeps her shrine, 'And Cupids ride the Lyon of the Deeps'. The Virgilian and Ovidian references are enriched by seeing this line not only as a grotesque parody of Arion on the dolphin's back, but as an anticipation of the infant's future 'posterity'—'the sons of sons of sons of whores'. The 'dauntless infant' is the antithesis of civilization as the true poet would have it, and the anti-type of the inspired singer (including Pope himself). Accordingly, such a passage has implications for Pope's complex tone in describing that final 'all-composing hour'. The 'dauntless infant' could not have been Dulness's spokesman because he is, literally (however shameless about it), unable to speak or utter. With him as hero-poet, there could have been no poem; whereas the true poet's triumph over Dulness consists, paradoxically, in his being able to write such a poem.

Here again the apparent shortcomings of the criticism have the capacity to stimulate a fruitful kind of argument, for Johnson is a critic who, even when we disagree with him, forces us to get clear the grounds of our dissent. The positive strengths, too, of his criticism are obvious enough, and derive from his full and intelligent engagement with particular works and authors. Because it represents what Leavis once aptly described as 'a powerful and distinguished mind operating at firsthand upon literature',[16] Johnson's criticism has outlived its century and justly earned the status of a classic.

[16] 'Johnson as Critic', *Scrutiny*, 12, No. 3 (Summer 1944), p. 187.

V

The Reciprocities of Style: Literary Criticism and Literary Statistics[1]

J.F. BURROWS

I

Those literary scholars who seek to identify the author of a disputed text or to set an undated text at the proper point in a chronological sequence are relying increasingly on statistical analysis and on the computer-assistance that facilitates it. But literary critics have found less use for such techniques. The objects of this paper are to show that statistical analysis can be addressed to questions which literary critics have customarily regarded as important and that it can advance our understanding in areas where conclusive answers are few and far between. To propose these objects is not to confuse means with ends. Statistical analysis is only a sophisticated method of comparison. And, as Johnson argues in the *Preface to Shakespeare*, comparison enriches but can never supplant the considered judgement in which literary criticism ultimately consists.

The questions I have chiefly in mind bear on the concepts of 'character' and 'narrative'; on interrelationships between them in the novels of Jane Austen (and some others); and on the ways in which value-judgements of a novel can be closely, if not simply, linked with the nuances of its language. Even when it is used only to gather the instances of a particular phenomenon, the computer can be helpful in stylistic analysis. Far beyond that, it offers the only feasible means of analysing the subtly varied patterns of frequency which obtain among the most common word-types of all and which make the groundwork of my argument. The present paper deals rather

[1] The research on which this paper draws could not have been conducted without the generous support of the Australian Research Grants Scheme; the University of Newcastle (NSW); the Cambridge Literary and Linguistic Computing Centre; and St John's College, Cambridge. Nor would it have been possible without access to the Oxford Concordance Package (OCP) and MINITAB (University of Pennsylvania) and without the advice and assistance of many friends and colleagues.

with results than with the underlying procedures. A more complete
account is given in my forthcoming monograph, *Computation into
Criticism: A Study of Jane Austen's Novels and an Experiment in Method*
(Oxford, Clarendon Press, forthcoming 1986).

'I' is the most common word in the dialogue of Jane Austen's
novels and in the 'idiolects' of most of her characters. But for some of
them it ranks second. For Collins and Tom Bertram, it ranks third.
And, for Henry Tilney, it ranks only sixth. Within one or another of
the idiolects, the topmost place is taken by each of the next five
words in the overall rank-order. As further comparisons of this kind
are added, it emerges that the whole rank-order of the very common
words differs from character to character. The following small table
shows a few of the more striking differences and shows that each of
the eight most common words can occupy almost any situation in
the upper ranges of the rank-order. (A similar 'mobility' obtains for
almost every word that occurs more than a hundred times in Jane
Austen's dialogue.)

	I	the	you	and	of	to (inf.)	a	it
OVERALL RANKING	1	2	3	4	5	6	7	8
Catherine Morland	1	7	2	5	8	6	12	4
Henry Tilney	6	1	2	4	3	7	5	11
John Thorpe	1	4	3	7	6	10	2	5
Collins	3	2	7	4	1	6	13	15
Mrs Gardiner	2	6	10	5	3	1	12	7=
Sir Thomas	2	5	1	4	3	6	8	13
Tom Bertram	3	2	7	1	5	10	4	6
Harriet Smith	1	8	4	2	10=	5	9	3

So great is the frequency with which these words occur that, taken
together, the eight of them amount to almost a fifth of all Jane
Austen's dialogue. (They range down from 11,910 instances of 'I' to
5659 instances of 'it' and amount to 60,177 words out of a dialogue-
total of 307,360 for the six novels.) So marked are the discrepancies
of ranking that (even when all of Jane Austen's major characters are
compared) they easily meet the requirements of any of the usual tests
of statistical 'significance'. The evidence of a striking and diverse
patterning is inescapable: the question is not whether it is meaningful
but what kind of meaning attaches to it.

One straightforward, revealing, but limited line of analysis
consists in taking any one (or any small set) of these words and,

guided by the statistical discrepancies, examining what the major characters actually make of it. An uncommonly strong (or weak) recourse to 'I' or 'you' on the one hand, to 'a' or 'the' on the other, admits *verifiable* inferences about different characters' habitual topics and their 'attitudes' to those topics. Striking contrasts of rank in words like 'and' and 'of' suggest that Jane Austen's characters differ as much from each other in their habitual syntactical patterns as they differ in attitude and topic. No speaker of a recognizable form of English can well avoid such words entirely: but an unusually marked recourse to (or avoidance of) any of them must affect the shape of all he says. Such effects are strengthened by the fact that a marked recourse to a particular word is almost always concentrated on only one or two of its various meanings or functions—on 'and', for example, as a connective of loose *or* well-knit clauses, *or* as a connective of particular sorts of phrase, *or* as a connective of proper names. Especially in recent years, this kind of analysis of single words and cognate analyses of small 'strings' of words have yielded some impressive findings in cases of disputed authorship.

And yet, even though some important facets of meaning are associated with the discrete properties of particular words and can usefully be approached in the manner sketched above, 'meaning' lies rather in the *patterning* of a language. At its broadest, that patterning may be construed, on Saussurean lines, as a system of relationships between '*la langue*' and '*la parole*', between the whole set of resources notionally available to all speakers of a language and the more limited set of choices actually adopted by a particular speaker. To the extent that the very common words share in that patterning and convey that larger, though less visible, dimension of meaning, we shall learn less from an analysis of 'I' or 'the' or 'and' as discrete phenomena than from a study of their reciprocities. If the little table set out above is examined in this way, there are signs of systematic difference between Collins and Harriet Smith, between Henry Tilney and Catherine Morland, and so on. When 'I' and 'you' rank high, 'of', 'the', and 'a' tend to fall away; and vice-versa. If this is enough to suggest a contrast between highly personal and more impersonal forms of speech, less simple contrasts begin to appear when John Thorpe, Mrs Gardiner, and Sir Thomas Bertram are considered. To put it loosely, then, a strong leaning towards some words will entail a leaning away from others. It is possible, however, to put it precisely: for these hidden reciprocities are persistent enough to distinguish one idiolect from another, exact enough to bring the idiolects into telling patterns of resemblance and contrast, and subtle enough to show appropriate changes in an idiolect as circumstances change.

The statistics of correlation offer simple ways of analysing the reciprocities in such sets of mutually dependent variables. Spearman's method treats directly of relationships in rank-order, like those given in the table, and yields reliable results. But Pearson's product-moment method allows, in addition, for differing 'gaps' between rank and rank. Whereas Mrs Gardiner's first five words ('to', 'I', 'of', 'he', and 'and') occur almost equally often Catherine Morland's first word ('I') occurs almost twice as often as her second ('you'), with the next two ('not' and 'it') lying close behind, and the fifth ('a') much further off again. In order to give this additional feature its due place, Pearson's method will be used throughout this paper and applied to the raw word-frequencies. In order to offer a broader cross-section of Jane Austen's dialogue, the thirty most common words (amounting to about 40% of the whole) will be analysed instead of the 20% made up by the eight most common words. (It should be noted, however, that very similar results flow from an analysis of the 20%, the 40%, and from the 50% made up by the sixty most common words. The underlying reciprocities are both consistent and pervasive.)

When it is employed in this way, Pearson's formula yields a correlation-coefficient of only 0.408 between Collins and Harriet Smith and, at the other extreme, a coefficient of 0.973 between Elizabeth Bennet and Emma Woodhouse. When each major idiolect is correlated with every other, the results form a convincing array of resemblances and contrasts. With the telling exception of Fanny Price, the heroes and heroines of Jane Austen's later novels all correlate closely with each other. The resemblances between Isabella Thorpe, Lucy Steele, Mrs Bennet, and her beloved Lydia are as close as each of them deserves. Sir Thomas Bertram has much more in common with Lady Catherine de Bourgh than with his wife, who finds a companion in Harriet Smith. Tom Bertram, Mr Weston, and Admiral Croft make up another little group.

But a hit-or-miss commentary like this does scant justice to the complex patterns of a correlation-matrix made up of the 1128 coefficients yielded when those forty-eight of Jane Austen's characters who speak two thousand or more words apiece are each correlated with the other forty-seven. It is better to 'map' the results and place each character in relation to all the rest. Such maps can be derived in several ways. 'Eigen-analysis', perhaps the most suitable for our purposes, reduces a matrix to a series of 'eigen-vectors'. The first vector arrays the set of cases—for us, the group of characters—in an order that represents the most consistent pattern of coefficients. The second vector offers the most consistent *residual* pattern, and so on. The results also include an indication of the relative weight of each successive vector, expressed as a percentage. When the first two or three vectors account for 90% and more of the whole shape of the original matrix, the array can usefully be 'mapped' in graphs like those that follow. In the course of many trials, I have not encountered a case where the results were too diffuse to yield a well delineated map.

A final process, known as 'cluster analysis', assigns precise statistical significance to the results. But maps like those that follow speak so plainly for their own meaningfulness that I think it unnecessary to complicate the issue. Cluster analysis would certainly be necessary if the method sketched above were applied to less familiar material than Jane Austen's novels, to less recognizable speakers than her major characters, or to documents whose authenticity lay in question.

II

The following graphs show a little of what issues from these methods of analysis. The two parts of Graph 1 are best thought of as two projections—floor-plan and side-elevation—of a transparent box. The second elevation shows, for instance, that (despite such resemblances as a habit of self-reference) Fanny Price, Frank Churchill, and Mary Musgrove differ sharply in other ways. Edmund and the Crawfords, on the other hand, are close neighbours in both projections.

Graph 1 is confined to Jane Austen's last three novels and treats of the characters who speak more than two thousand words apiece. The exclusion of the first three novels clarifies the picture by removing the evidence of a chronological development in Jane Austen's dialogue: when those other characters are included, many of them lie towards or even beyond the edges of the present floor-plan. The characters of Jane Austen's three Chawton novels, that is to say, are less obviously contrasted with each other than their predecessors had been.

When both projections of the map are held in mind, it not only

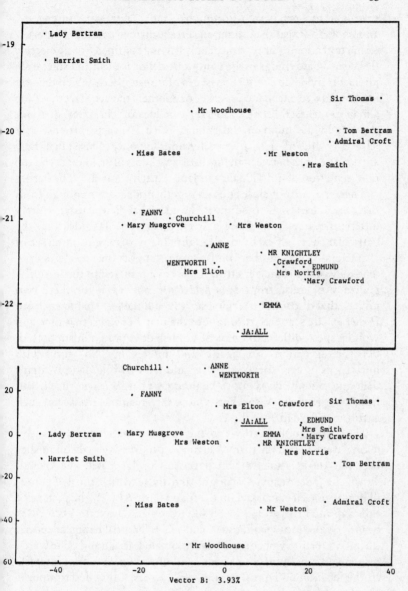

Graph 1: Major Characters of Jane Austen's Last Three
Novels

(Word-types 1–30 of her Dialogue)

reveals some persuasive groupings (and a few very interesting anomalies) but also sheds light on certain current attitudes to literary characterization. Since the analysis is confined to objective frequency–patternings in the commonest words of all and since each idiolect is made up of those passages of direct speech which the text itself assigns to one named speaker or another, the very fact that such a map can be established shows that the idea of 'character' does not *originate* in the mind of the reader. (That is not to propose that 'character' and 'idiolect' are synonymous but only to insist that there are definite links between the stylistic attributes of an idiolect and the representation of individuality in Jane Austen's novels.) The heroes and heroines are not close enough together or separate enough from the other characters to support the idea that Jane Austen chiefly differentiates between those general categories. The idea that the particular 'note' of each novel might chiefly distinguish one set of characters from another finds some support in the 'westerly' tendency of the characters from *Emma* as compared to the 'easterly' tendency of those from *Mansfield Park*: but, even for these two novels, that distribution is not uniform; and the five characters from *Persuasion* are scattered throughout the map. The idea that men and women speak different brands of English does not go unsupported: but the exceptions are many and interesting. So, too, with differences of age, social standing, and familial rôle. Jane Austen's dialogue, obviously, is not to be thought of as '*la langue*' itself. But her dialogue treats of speakers whose interrelations transcend such extrinsic differentiae as these.

The actual configurations of the map are better understood by taking each vector in turn. Vector A progressively distinguishes between those idiolects which most closely match the overall 'norm' of Jane Austen's dialogue and those which most diverge. (The norm itself is marked on the map as 'JA: ALL'.) The pattern of this map and many others like it suggests that to traverse Vector B is to move from loose, colloquial, and self-referential habits of speech through a territory of comparatively 'normal' usage and on towards more firmly disciplined, 'correct', and impersonal kinds of idiolect. (If the location of Tom Bertram seems to resist that description, it should be remembered that he has most to say during his father's absence, when he speaks as the incipient baronet.) The meaning of Vector C changes from map to map. But, in Graph 1, the array runs from the interlocutory style of those who lie near the lower extremity to the disquisitory style of those who lie near the top. Fanny Price often speaks sententiously and at length when she dares to speak at all. The shape of Frank Churchill's idiolect is greatly influenced by the comparatively unconversational properties of his long letter to Mrs Weston. The small speaking-parts of Anne and Wentworth are dominated by their long retrospective comments. Towards the opposite extremity, only Miss Bates is much given to speaking at length: but, if lengthy speeches of that sort are a sign of intellectual discipline, it is the author's.

In treating idiolects as if each could be assigned to a fixed location, Graph 1 does less than justice to Jane Austen's capacity to portray the processes of change. Change, for some characters, is no more than a shift from a conversational to an epistolary mode. For others, like Mrs Norris, the changes have to do with differences of conversational relationship: consider how differently she addresses Sir Thomas, Lady Bertram, and her unfortunate youngest niece. And for others again, especially the later heroes and heroines, change consists in sustained and appropriate development. These various kinds of change tend to produce an 'averaging-effect' when a whole idiolect is subjected to analysis; and the effect is to carry the more dynamic idiolects towards the general norm. Graph 1 serves best, therefore, as an overall sketch—and as a more adequate picture of those comparatively unchanging idiolects that stand at its extremities.

In Graph 2, which is composed in the same fashion as the first projection of Graph 1, the major characters of *Mansfield Park* are matched with those of *The Waves* and Georgette Heyer's *Frederica*. As might be expected, the solitary reveries of Bernard, Jinny, and the rest are far removed from the more conversational idiolects of the other two novels; but, even with those two novels, the main clusters of idiolects stand well apart.

The fact that Vector B bears much more weight here than it did in Graph 1—15% as against 4%—shows that the contrast between intellectual discipline and looseness distinguishes even more sharply among these three groups of speakers than when three groups of Jane Austen's speakers were compared. Except for Charles Trevor, the characters of *Frederica* all lie near or beyond Lady Bertram's extreme position on the horizontal axis.[2] The exception actually adds weight

[2] Because they depend upon the precise distribution of the data, the polarities of apparently similar eigen-maps (like Graphs 1 and 2) are sometimes inverted. Yet the essential point is not whether Lady Bertram, for example, lies at the eastern extremity or the western but that she lies at the opposite extremity from Sir Thomas. The patterns treat of relativities.

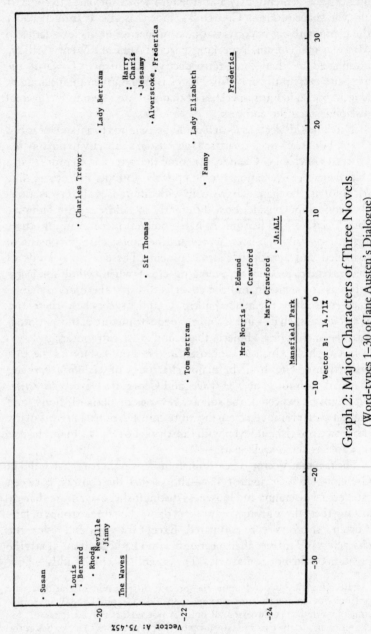

Graph 2: Major Characters of Three Novels
(Word-types 1–30 of Jane Austen's Dialogue)

to this demonstration that Georgette Heyer's characters speak comparatively loosely. For Charles Trevor has very little to say save when he offers a carefully marshalled 'history' of an abortive elopement. The effect of this single long discourse is enough to isolate him in Graph 2 (and, indeed, to carry him some way towards the territory occupied by Willoughby and Colonel Brandon, Jane Austen's chief 'historians', when their idiolects are included).

The narrator of *Frederica* insists on the individuality of the characters. In the dialogue of the novel, however, they are differentiated rather by little tricks of speech—oaths here and polite exclamations there—than by those more fundamental stylistic traits which distinguish Jane Austen's characters from each other. (It should be recognized, moreover, that the diversity of Jane Austen's characters is even greater than Graph 2 suggests: since their idiolects are much more responsive to the processes of change, they 'average down' more markedly than those of *Frederica* or *The Waves*.)

Graph 2 shows, in short, that the frequency-patterning of the very common words is enough not only to set the characters of different novelists in distinct 'authorial' clusters but also to indicate that Jane Austen's are the most sharply differentiated, one from another. In so far as *Mansfield Park* and *Frederica* rely on the individualization of character, Jane Austen makes more versatile use of the basic resources of the language. *The Waves*, however, is too different in kind to admit so plain a value judgement.

Graph 3 treats of Jane Austen's six novels and offers a contrast between dialogue and two forms of narrative, a contrast so uniform and powerful that Vectors A and B account for more than 98% of the overall effect. This graph differs from the first two in being derived from a modified word-list. When the thirty most common words are all included, the deictic words—especially the personal pronouns and the inflected auxiliary verbs—throw all the emphasis on the difference between direct and indirect speech. When the deictic words are excluded and more subdued differences are allowed their full effect, the contrast between dialogue and narrative not only survives but calls for subtler kinds of explanation.

Although the terms are mine, the contrast between 'pure narrative' and 'character narrative' is familiar to Jane Austen's readers. The latter is made up of all those passages in which the unspoken thoughts of a character are rendered as if at first hand. The former is that much larger, 'impersonal' constituent of the novels which incorporates everything from scene-setting and narrative-mechanics

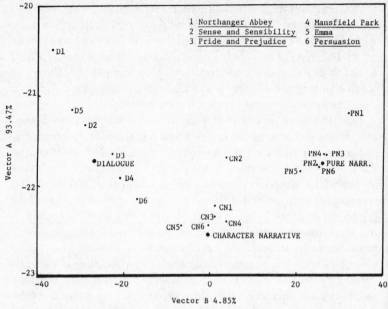

Graph 3: Major Constituents of Jane Austen's Novels

(Non-deictic word-types 1–18 of her Literary Vocabulary)

to the outward description of the characters' ideas. The separating out of the two main forms of narrative rests on no firmer ground than my considered judgement of the little signals with which Jane Austen supplies the attentive reader. But the fact that 'pure narrative' and 'character narrative' make such discrete clusters in the map shows that a multitude of particular decisions can yield an acceptable result.

The most aberrant entry in the map is 'CN2', the character narrative of *Sense and Sensibility*. In that somewhat stilted early novel, the narrative has much to say of what Elinor is thinking but does not often render the processes of her thought. Even *Northanger Abbey* is more sophisticated in this respect: the need to 'distance' Catherine's wilder fancies calls for a more sustained form of character narrative than Elinor's. The last three novels offer subtler and more pervasive interconnections between the thoughts of the heroines and the things they say. The six pure narratives are closely grouped except that a vigorous 'authorial' commentary—on heroines, novels, life in Bath, and the ultimate 'tendency of this work'—carries the pure narrative of *Northanger Abbey* (PN1) into territory where, in a more general map, the highly discursive narrative of *Howards End* also finds a place. The comparatively wide spread of the dialogue cluster arises from the fact that, as we have seen, the dialogue of each novel is a compound of distinctive idiolects.

The chief interest of Graph 3, then, is as evidence that the major constituents of the novels fall into discrete and well-knit clusters. This line of analysis can be developed by mapping each cluster separately. When that is done with the pure narratives, they align themselves in what is generally regarded as their proper chronological order, from *Northanger Abbey* to *Persuasion*. The reason is that the very correlation coefficients register a progressive relaxation, familiar to attentive readers, of the strict Augustan discipline of Jane Austen's early prose. When the character narratives of Fanny, Emma, and Anne Elliot are separated from the rest, it is possible to compare 'speech idiolects' and 'thought idiolects'. With Fanny and Emma, the results make for illuminating contrasts between two facets of each 'literary personality'. With Anne, especially, the two idiolects converge.

Graphs 4 and 5 show two ways of illustrating the processes of change. In order to deal in sufficiently high word frequencies to admit sensible analysis, they treat only of idiolects that exceed six thousand words apiece and draw only on the twelve most common word-types. (Those twelve amount, nevertheless, to a quarter of each idiolect.)

Graph 4 is concise but crude, showing how successive phases of an idiolect conform to its overall frequency-patterning. It does *not* show, for example, when Fanny most resembles Edmund or Mary but only when Fanny is 'most herself' or least so. Despite that limitation, it shows that the idiolects of Jane Austen's characters change far more vigorously than those of Georgette Heyer, Virginia Woolf, or James. Most of the main idiolects in all Jane Austen's novels, except for *Northanger Abbey*, change at least as much as those of Edmund and Mary. Only Marianne Dashwood and Mr Knightley change as radically as Fanny Price.

A closer inspection of Graph 4 yields the beginnings of an insight into the dramatic shape of each novel. At the time of the visit to Sotherton and the rehearsing of *Lovers' Vows*, when Fanny is least herself, Mary and Edmund are most themselves. When she recovers herself, they (especially Mary) are most at odds with themselves. A similar patterning, in low relief, can be discerned in *The Awkward*

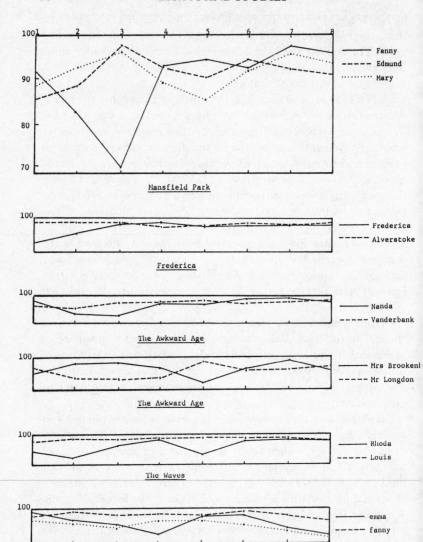

Graph 4: Patterns of Variation within Some Major Idiolects

(Word-types 1–12 of Jane Austen's Dialogue in top five diagrams; non-deictic word-types 1–12 in bottom diagram)

Age; and it appears not only in the two leading couples represented here but also, even more clearly, in the Duchess and Mitchy. It is obviously appropriate that Mr Longdon and Mrs Brookenham should lose themselves and recover themselves in so symmetrical an interchange. And, given that the genteel savagery of Mrs Brook's *salon* makes it wise for all of them to conceal their true thoughts and feelings, it is still more appropriate that the secondary characters should betray themselves by franker speaking (and therefore change more obviously) than Vanderbank and Nanda allow themselves. Except in the opening chapters, where Frederica tells Alverstoke the history of her family, the idiolects of *Frederica* scarcely change at all. The changes in the idiolects of *The Waves*, at their strongest in Rhoda and their weakest in poor frozen Louis, are much slighter than those of Jane Austen's 'speech-idiolects'. But when these idiolects are compared, more aptly, with the 'thought-idiolects' of Jane Austen's last three heroines, it can be seen that they change in much the same degree.

Whereas Graph 4 treats correlation-coefficients as if they were consecutive entries in a temperature-chart, Graph 5 is an eigen-map of the changing conversational relationship between Emma and Mr Knightley. It is based not on the whole idiolect of either character but on 'sub-idiolects' comprising only those words which each addresses to the other. (A full analysis of her sub-idiolects shows that, whereas Emma originally employs somewhat different conversational styles for different people, the process of self-discovery rendered in this novel consists, in part, in the emergence of a more homogeneous idiolect.) Graph 5 shows that change can amount to a vigorous and sustained line of development. Emma and Mr Knightley begin (at AB1 and BA1 respectively) at a distance from each other and an even greater distance from 'JA: ALL'. As their disagreements intensify, they move even further from 'normality' and Mr Knightley, especially, enters into territory occupied by Sir Thomas and by Henry Tilney at his most didactic. But, as they gradually find common ground and discover their underlying *rapport*, the distance between them diminishes. At the same time they approach those less strident ways of speaking which support the idea that Emma's character has developed and that Mr Knightley can at last (though not at first) be granted the 'normative' function assigned to him by so many critics of *Emma*.

Few modern literary critics, few modern intellectuals, believe, with Samuel Johnson, that the exercise of judgement may ultimately

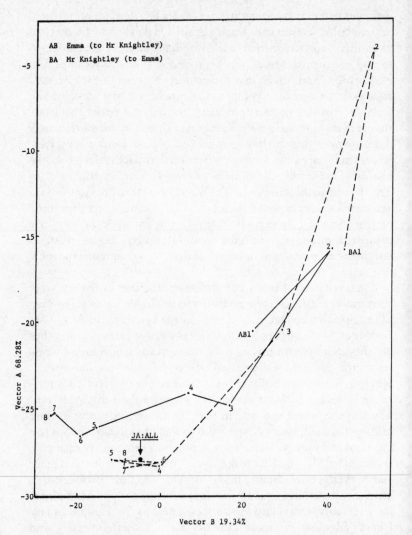

Graph 5: Changing Patterns of Conversation between Emma and Mr Knightley

(Word-types 1–12 of Jane Austen's Dialogue, including their contracted forms)

allow 'the mind [to] repose on the stability of truth'. However honestly and impartially we try to proceed, the very questions that we choose to put condition the answers that emerge. Those answers lead, in turn, to endlessly receding questions. To what extent, for example, do my findings testify to a genuine individuality in Jane Austen's characters? To what extent do they depend upon the 'dialogic relationships' enunciated by Formalists like Bakhtin? To what extent does the (frequent but not universal) convergence of related idiolects reflect that 'accommodation theory' whereby those who talk much with each other come to talk much like each other? To what extent does the 'core-grammar' of Chomsky's recent work lie at the heart of the whole system of reciprocities? Such questions are canvassed in my forthcoming book: but, even if they were exhausted, still others would arise.

Such value as attaches to my findings will chiefly rest, therefore, on the extent to which they encourage others to pursue fresh questions of their own. More immediately, however, even the evidence of this paper may cast some little doubt on the current predilection for binary forms of definition and the 'privileging' of more or less factitious categories—cooked *or* raw, lexical or grammatical, paradigmatic or syntagmatic, Aryan or Rastaferian, moon-female or sun-male. Such methods, perhaps, are better suited to open-and-shut cases than to the complexities of literature. Although statistical methods of comparison, on the other hand, may seem 'mechanical', they are at a clear advantage in treating of all the small but meaningful gradations that lie between extremes, in recognizing that no extreme is absolute, and in avoiding Procrustean beds. The evidence offered in this paper also suggests that the empirical emphasis of 'close reading' is well founded. That proposition rests not only on the fact that so many of the results sketched here are in keeping with the ideas of Jane Austen's most respected critics—the best (or best known) of her readers. It also rests on the fact that good readers are capable of discriminations too fine to be registered as 'statistically significant'. Elizabeth and Emma, the figures indicate, are more alike than any other pair of Jane Austen's speakers. To read a series of appropriate passages attentively is to recognize the force of that result—but also to recognize subtle differences enough to prevent either from being mistaken for the other.

VI

Blake and the Natural History of Creation

ANDREW LINCOLN

I

Blake's imaginative investigation of human origins placed him in a curious, partial alignment with those thinkers of the Enlightenment who sought to replace the Biblical cosmographic tradition with science. Blake, of course, had no wish to elevate scientific explanation over the sublime allegories of the Bible or *Paradise Lost*. But he wrote from a perspective that embraced not only myth but also rationalistic and naturalistic views that would normally be regarded as alien or hostile to myth. Many of the obscurities of Blake's first visionary epic, *The Four Zoas*, arise not from the use of obscure sources, but from an extraordinary interplay of contrasting views of human origins, in which elements derived from familiar mythical texts—notably from *Paradise Lost*—appear in an unfamiliar form. In this essay I should like to explore this interplay as it appears in the account of creation developed in the first two books, or 'Nights', of Blake's 'Dream of Nine Nights'.

Compared with the predominantly negative view of creation dramatized in *The First Book of Urizen*, Blake's later comments on this subject seem ambivalent. In the prose commentary on 'The Last Judgement' (1810) he wrote:

> Many suppose that before the Creation All was Solitude & Chaos This is the most pernicious Idea that can enter the Mind as it takes away all sublimity from the Bible & Limits All Existence to Creation & to Chaos To the Time & Space fixed by the Corporeal Vegetative Eye ... Eternity Exists and All things in Eternity Independent of Creation which was an act of mercy.[1]

The passage brings into focus a paradox that assumed a central importance in Blake's thought. In his cosmography, the vision of a

---

[1] *The Complete Poetry and Prose of William Blake*, ed. David V. Erdman with commentary by Harold Bloom (New York, 1982), p. 563. All quotations of Blake come from this edition. Deletions signalled in the text are omitted.

created universe is the consequence of humanity's lapse from the active mental life of eternity: succumbing to the 'female will' Blake's Eternal Man, Albion, falls into the belief that nature has an objective existence. The created universe is therefore a delusion that must be exploded. But as the vision of a created universe redeems man from a less coherent vision of his environment, the act of creation is seen as an act of mercy, as an expression of the divinely creative potential of the human mind. Blake thus embraces two apparent contraries. In 1803 or 1804, he began to introduce to his mythology a number of devices that expressed these contrary views directly and separately.[2] But the imagery and narrative sequence of *The Four Zoas* is shaped fundamentally by the convergence of these contraries, and it is the effect of the convergence that I shall examine here.

II

In the light of Blake's complex attitude, the providential conception of creation, presented in such vibrant detail in *Paradise Lost*, would seem to be a partial vision of the truth. It needs to be qualified by a perspective which shows that all ideas about the creation of a material universe originate in man's fallen perceptions. Paradoxically, although Blake regards nature as a delusion, his investigation of the modes of perception that condition religious ideas is in some respects naturalistic; the ideas that imprison the fallen mind are seen as the 'natural' expression of a particular level of consciousness ('fixed by the Corporeal Vegetative Eye'). In *The Four Zoas* the naturalistic perspective offers a view of the development of religion that has some similarities with views expressed by Hume in his essay *The Natural History of Religion* (1757).[3] Hume argues that

[2] He opposes, for example, the activities of the Daughters of Albion (who control Albion's 'vegetative powers') to the activities of Los the Eternal prophet. And he introduces a higher redemptive agency, the 'Council of God', which in its collective form is identified as Jesus, and from which the redemptive structures and initiatives that will rescue Albion from his fallen condition are ultimately derived.

[3] *The Natural History of Religion and Dialogues concerning Natural Religion* by David Hume, ed. A. Wayne Colver and John Valdimir Price (Oxford, 1976). All quotations of Hume are taken from this edition. Many scholars have noted that Blake's views of the development of religion are in some respects similar to those widely held by mythographers and Deists in the eighteenth century. See for example Ruthven Todd, *Tracks in the Snow* (London, 1946). Hume's approach seems more naturalistic and more provocative than that of many of his English contemporaries.

while a belief in a supreme creator has its foundation in reason, the most ancient, polytheistic religions have their origins 'in human nature' (p. 25). The ancient mythologists did not consider their deities to be the conscious creators of the universe. Primitive man (so unlike Milton's Adam, as Hume insists) had little leisure for detached contemplation of the physical universe. Instead, the ancient mythologists, casting the world in their own image, 'seem thoughout to have rather embraced the idea of generation than that of creation, or formation; and to have thence accounted for the origin of this universe' (p. 42). 'Generation' refers to the idea that natural phenomena originally came into being through the sexual activities of the gods, an idea that appears for example in Hesiod's *Theogony*. In Hume's view, the primitive mind rises gradually from polytheism to theism 'by abstracting from what is imperfect', according to the 'natural progress of human thought' (p. 27). By implication, the perception of design in the universe, and the belief in a supreme creator, are characteristic of the more reflective consciousness of more advanced civilizations. Blake's myth in the opening Nights of *The Four Zoas* embodies a comparable distinction between the generated world of the primitive mind and the designed cosmos of civilization. Here, however, the distinction forms the basis of an intricate reconstruction of Milton's myth of creation.[4]

In *Paradise Lost* Milton defines the relationship of creator to creation in two rather different ways. The creator is first seen as a detached architect, setting limits to the universe with the precision (and one of the instruments) of a mathematician:

> . . . in his hand
> He took the golden Compasses, prepar'd
> In Gods Eternal store, to circumscribe
> This Universe, and all created things:
> One foot he center'd, and the other turn'd
> Round through the vast profunditie obscure,
> And said, 'thus farr extend, thus farr thy bounds,
> This be thy just Circumference, O World.'
> (VII.224–31, p. 219)[5]

---

[4] For a different view of Blake's use of *Paradise Lost* in these Nights see Jackie DiSalvo, *War of Titans* (Pittsburgh, 1983), pp. 101–235.

[5] *The Works of John Milton*, ed. Frank Allen Patterson, *et al.*, 20 vols (New York, 1931) II.219. All quotations from *Paradise Lost* are taken from this edition.

This image would seem to account for the principles of order and proportion manifest in the symmetrical form and harmonious revolutions of the spheres, principles that give the heavens the character of a perfectly tuned mechanism turning on its 'great axel'. The second image of the creator as the Spirit of God suggests a more intimate relationship between creator and creation:

> . . . on the watrie calme
> His brooding wings the Spirit of God outspred,
> And vital vertue infus'd, and vital warmth
> Throughout the fluid Mass.   (VII.234–7, p. 220)

This view of creation would seem to account for the internal energies manifest in the evolution of the earth and in the generation of organic life. In Milton's poem 'two great Sexes animate the world' (VIII.148–51, p. 220). In response to the divine command, life on earth issues from the sexual union of earth and sea: the 'Main Ocean' fertilizes the 'Embryon' earth in the 'Womb of Waters' (VII.276–284, p. 221); organic life-forms burst vigorously from the womb of the earth in a spontaneous generation. In elaborating the creation myth of Genesis 1, then, Milton accounts at once for the organic vitality of the earth and for the mechanical precision of the heavens by combining the imagery of generation and of design.

For Blake, as for Hume, the perception of the world as a generated organism, and the perception of it as an intricately designed cosmos, have their bases in two quite different aspects of consciousness. Indeed, in Blake's myth the distinction appears to reflect the fundamental dissociation of sensible and intelligible qualities that is inherent in the perception of an object world. This division in experience is dramatized in the relationship between Tharmas (associated with the flux of the sensible world) and Urizen (creator of the abstract patterns of the intellect). Hence Tharmas and Urizen are the two agents of creation in the opening Nights of *The Four Zoas*. In Blake's account of their activities the imagery of generation and the imagery of design are separated, and express two distinct phases in the development of the fallen mind.

Blake's myth of creation properly begins, as Milton's does, with the circumscription of chaos. As the 'Eternal Man' Albion withdraws from eternity, allowing his mind to become passive, he lapses into the perception of nature—in which all life will seem to be governed by the automatic cycles of growth and decay. The perception of the cyclical form of nature provides a limit to the potential chaos of Albion's fall, but does not in itself suggest a design in the physical universe. Thus in Blake's myth, chaos is circumscribed not by mathematical design, but by the inherent shaping power of the senses—that is, by Tharmas, the power that controls Man's sensations in the active mental life of Eternity:

> Tharmas groand among his Clouds . . .
> And stretching out his holy hand in the vast Deep sublime
> Turnd round the circle of Destiny with tears & bitter sighs
> (5:8,10–11, p. 302)

Enion, the female counterpart or emanation of Tharmas, is the embodiment of his world-view. As the mind becomes passive, Tharmas—separated from Enion—loses control of the sensations he should organize and is overwhelmed by them. Thus Tharmas actually sinks down into the waters of Albion's disorganized consciousness and is himself completely submerged in them. Milton's image of the creator as a divine spirit that moves on the face of the waters and allows his creative influence to be absorbed by them is transformed into an image of the fall.

From this point Blake's myth appears to offer an account of the natural history of human consciousness in a way that parallels the development of the infant mind.[6] The account is remarkable in its detail and apparent precision. First the mind is powerless to distinguish between its sensations and exists in a state of disorganized unity—Tharmas is submerged in the woof of Enion. Consciousness must now develop in relation to a world that is perceived as external. As the mind is passively stimulated it gradually becomes aware of this object world—Enion weaves the Spectre of Tharmas in her loom, and as the 'circle of Destiny' is completed, the world begins to take apprehensible form: 'Round rolld the Sea Englobing in a watry Globe self balancd / A Frowning Continent appeared' (5:25–6, pp. 302–3). A sense of individual identity develops, and the growing mind is stimulated into active engagement with its environment—the Spectre rises and attempts to dominate Enion. Through this encounter the primal integrity of consciousness is lost as experience consolidates into a sharper

---

[6] I am particularly indebted here to Peter Fisher's account of the fall of Tharmas in *The Valley of Vision* (Toronto, 1961), p. 232.

perception of time and space—the Spectre is absorbed by Enion, a union that results in the birth of Los and Enitharmon, who control the awareness of time and space respectively.

The implicit connection made by Milton between the creative power of the Spirit of God and the sexual generation of nature is made explicit in the myth of Tharmas: the biblical image of the spirit of god moving on the waters introduces a 'primitive' myth of generation that expresses the primal drives and intimate engagement characteristic of the early stages of human consciousness. Each new stage of perception is imaged as a new stage of creation. In the original draft of Blake's poem, organic life-forms finally appeared at the birth of Los and Enitharmon in a passage that parallels in miniature the magnificent descriptions of spontaneous generation in *Paradise Lost*:

The barked Oak, the long limbd Beech; the Ches'nut tree; the Pine.
The Pear tree mild, the frowning Walnut, the sharp Crab & Apple sweet,
The rough bark opens; twittering peep forth little beaks & wings
The Nightingale, the Goldfinch, Robin, Lark, Linnet & Thrush
The Goat leap'd from the craggy cliff, the Sheep awoke from the mould
Upon its green stalk rose the Corn, waving innumerable.

(p. 824)[7]

Blake's use of *Paradise Lost* frequently suggests that Milton's literal interpretation of the Bible provides—in its paradoxes and suppressed contradictions—an unintentional clarification of the Bible's imaginative significance. In Genesis 1, light is created on the first day, producing Day and Night, but not until the fourth day is this initial distinction refined, when God creates lights in the firmament of heaven. For Milton, who admits in *Christian Doctrine* that 'we cannot imagine light without some source of light,[8] this distinction poses a problem. His solution actually draws attention to the paradox: in his description of the first day of creation, Etherial light is 'Sphear'd in a radiant Cloud, for yet the Sun / Was not; she in a cloudie Tabernacle Sojourned the while' (VII.247–9). For Blake the distinction has a precise significance: it expresses two stages in

[7] Blake eventually deleted this passage in an extensive revision of the opening of his poem.
[8] *The Complete Prose Works of John Milton*, ed. Don M. Wolfe, *et al.*, 8 vols (New Haven and London, 1973), VI. 312.

the history of human perception. In the primitive phase, Albion's consciousness is dominated by Los and Enitharmon, the Adam and Eve of Blake's myth, who at this stage symbolize an unmethodized, childlike, imaginative perception of time and space. They experience 'times' and 'spaces' rather than Time and Space. Hence 'purple night' and 'golden day' appear, but 'the bright Sun was not as yet; he filling all the expanse / Slept as a bird in the blue shell that soon shall burst away' (12:38–9, p. 307). It is not until the creation of the cosmos, when Urizen reshapes Albion's perception of nature into an intelligible system, that a new consciousness of time and space begins to emerge, and light is related to particular sources in the heavenly bodies.

III

In Blake's account of the transition from the primitive world to the designed cosmos, the difference between the moral basis of his myth and that of *Paradise Lost* is brought into focus. At this point Blake's narrative offers a particularly close parallel with Milton's.

Milton's Adam, whose first impulse is to turn to the heavens, learns at the very dawn of consciousness that God is the author of the universe. But a full explanation of creation is given to him only when Satan has entered Eden. After Eve tells Adam of her dream, in which she was tempted to eat the fruit of the tree of knowledge and subsequently flew up to the clouds with her tempter, Raphael is commanded to descend to Eden and advise Adam of 'his happy state'. The placing of Raphael's account of creation emphasizes the moral significance of the perception of design in the universe, as a reinforcement against the encroachments of evil.

In Blake's view, evil does not intrude into the newly created world from without. Rather the creation itself is an embodiment of error that fosters delusions in the growing mind. In the light of this view, Eve's dream would appear to have a significance that Milton himself did not perceive. In *Paradise Lost* the dream foreshadows Eve's fall, but from Blake's point of view Adam and Eve are already fallen: female is separated from male, emanation exists remote from active mental power. Eve's dream of rising to a godlike existence is a characteristic expression of the female will, of that seductive power of the natural world that Albion succumbed to when he fell. It is also a recognition that human power is limited in the natural world—that humanity is indeed fallen. In Blake's myth this sense of limitation itself gives rise to Man's conviction that he is subject to the proscriptions of a divine power who will punish disobedience, and it stimulates the need to see a providential design in the world.

The myth of *The Four Zoas* reconstructs Milton's sequence on a new basis in order to clarify its latent or 'infernal' meaning. Los and Enitharmon, with none of the dignity of Milton's Adam and Eve, engage in a nomadic exploration that eventually leads them to the limits of their paradisal world: 'They wanderd long, till they sat down upon the margind sea' (9:32, p. 305). The ocean of sensory experience that initially overwhelmed the passive mind—'the sea of Time and Space' (56:13, p. 337)—remains because the fallen mind cannot reduce all of its sensations into apprehensible form. The arrival at this sea appears to symbolize the eventual confrontation of the growing mind with that part of experience usually regarded as the province of metaphysics. It is here that Los first names Enitharmon, just as in Genesis Adam first names Eve after she has eaten the forbidden fruit. And it is here that Enitharmon describes to Los her vision of the origin of Man's fall from eternity. In her 'Song of Death' she tells how the powers controlling the human passions attempt to dominate Albion's consciousness: 'Luvah and Vala woke & flew up from the Human Heart / Into the Brain; from thence upon the pillow Vala slumber'd' (10:11–12, p. 305). Enitharmon's dream thus reproduces in its own terms the upward flight of Eve's dream. It locates the fall in the usurpation of the passions, through which Man is seduced by the beauty of nature. Enitharmon's recognition that humanity is fallen stimulates in Los a sense of guilt and visions of divine punishment: 'I see the invisible knife / I see the shower of blood: I see the swords & spears of futurity' (11:13–14, p. 306).

The sequence suggests that as soon as the developing mind confronts the unknown, it becomes painfully aware of its fallen condition, and begins to develop a myth of its origins and destiny. Los and Enitharmon, who have a childlike simplicity, can safely rest on the 'margind sea' without being totally engulfed by it. They continue to perceive the world imaginatively, animating it with gods and spirits, as Blake thought the ancient poets had done (see *The Marriage of Heaven and Hell* 11, p. 38). But their speculations stimulate Urizen, the intellect—as yet unfallen—who descends from eternity at the conclusion of their exchanges as a prelude to his own act of creation. When Albion confronts the sea of time and space with his intellect, it seems an appalling void that threatens to overwhelm him. Hence Urizen must create a world view that will transform the blind revolutions of the 'circle of Destiny' into an intelligible system of belief.

In introducing his own account of the creation of the cosmos, then, Blake follows the sequence of Milton's myth closely: Urizen descends to the golden feast of Los and Enitharmon after they have begun to speculate about the fall, just as Raphael descends to the feast of Adam and Eve. Urizen's descent with ten thousand thousand hosts and glittering chariots recalls not only Raphael's descent to Eden, but also Milton's description of the Son coming to the task of creation.[9] There is no distinction between the revelation and the act of creation in Blake's myth: creation is a reorganization of human perceptions.

IV

After Urizen has descended, the generated world is replaced by the intricately designed cosmos of organized civilization. In Blake's myth, early civilization and the cosmos both originate in the intellect's horror of the void. Urizen's first task is to create the instruments—including the golden compasses—on which fallen civilizations must depend. From the natural point of view this appears to be a major advance, but from an eternal point of view it represents a new division in experience, a further separation of subject from object. Urizen's relationship with his creation is not primarily sexual, as Tharmas's was. Instead he creates as an architect, treating his experience objectively as raw material that can be shaped according to an impersonal will. The mathematical form of his universe is thus created at the expense of desire (Luvah is rigorously suppressed). Nevertheless, this cosmos is quite unlike the creation described in *The First Book of Urizen*. It is a work of seductive beauty, an impressive—if flawed—manifestation of the divine potential of the intellect, an imprisoning system which nevertheless provides in its mathematical precision the reassurance that has become necessary to the fallen mind. Blake's tone in describing it is heavily ambivalent:

> But infinitely beautiful the wondrous work arose
> In sorrow & care. a Golden World whose porches round the
> heavens

[9] Compare *The Four Zoas* 12:32–4, p. 307 and *Paradise Lost* VII.192–215, pp. 218–19.

And pillard halls & rooms recievd the eternal wandering stars
A wondrous golden Building; many a window many a door
And many a division let in & out into the vast unknown
Cubed in window square immoveable, within its walls & ceilings
The heavens were closd and spirits mournd their bondage night
  and day.

(32:7–13, p. 321)

The mixture of admiration and regret in this passage is one aspect of the interplay of contrary views, an interplay that shapes the myth as a whole. In Blake's poem the fallen mind arrives at the perception of design in creation as the consequence of a crisis that arises inevitably from Albion's lapse into the vision of nature. But this natural history of religion is dramatized in imagery derived from the best known account of a divine revelation in English poetry. Two types of explanation are evoked simultaneously, so that each may qualify the other. The natural history reveals the provisional nature of the cosmos, by showing its origin in man's fallen perceptions. The providential myth defines the status of creation, by showing it as an act of mercy, and by emphasizing the essential if fallen divinity of the human mind. Coleridge might not have envisaged such a balancing and reconciliation of opposites when he considered the creative activity of poets, but in *The Four Zoas* it is a characteristic expression of Blake's extraordinary imagination.

VII

Macaulay's Vision of 1930: Wordsworth and the Battle for the Wilderness

STEPHEN PRICKETT

In 1830 Thomas Babington Macaulay reviewed Southey's *Colloquies on Society* for the *Edinburgh Review*. By means of a series of conversations with the ghost of Sir Thomas More—now a time-traveller visiting the early nineteenth century—Southey had raised a whole group of urgent questions of the day: a group that were soon to be known under Carlyle's umbrella-term as 'the condition-of-England question'.[1] They included poverty, industrialization, Catholic emancipation, national education, emigration, the position of women, the growth of infidelity, and the spread of revolutionary ideas by printing. Above all, Southey attacked the economic and industrial system which, he claimed, profited the few and pauperized the many. In reply, Macaulay vigorously defends the doctrine of *laissez-faire*. He does not deny the 'present distresses' but, prompted perhaps by the spiritual presence of Henry VIII's one-time Lord Chancellor, he embarks on a survey of the economic history of England since Tudor times in order to show that 'in spite of all the misgovernment of her rulers' England 'has been almost constantly becoming richer and richer. Now and then there has been a stoppage, now and then a short regression; but as to the general tendency there can be no doubt. A single breaker may recede; but the tide is evidently coming in.'[2] He concludes by projecting the progress of the past into an England of a hundred years hence:

> If we were to prophesy that in the year 1930 a population of fifty millions, better fed, clad, and lodged than the English of our time, will cover these islands, that Sussex and Huntingdonshire will be wealthier than the wealthiest parts of the West Riding of Yorkshire now are, that cultivation, rich as that of a flower-garden, will be carried up to the very tops of Ben Nevis and

---

[1] The phrase seems to have been coined as the title to Chapter 1 of *Chartism* (1839).

[2] Macaulay, *Literary Essays* (Oxford, 1913), pp. 132–3.

Helvellyn, that machines constructed on principles yet
undiscovered, will be in every house, that there will be no
highways but railroads, no travelling but by steam, that our debt,
vast as it seems to us, will appear to our great-grandchildren a
trifling incumbrance, which might easily be paid off in a year or
two, many people would think us insane . . .[3]

Though Macaulay, frightened perhaps that his readers might take
him at his word, is quick to add 'we prophesy nothing . . .' the
passage is none the less a quite remarkable exercise in what is now
(*pace* Herman Kahn) called 'futurology'. From a population of 13.9
million (1831 census) Macaulay 'prophesies' a figure of 50 million:
the actual figure in the 1931 census was 46 million. We can forgive
him the hyperbole of 'no travelling but by steam', for he has grasped
the essential transformation of travel implied by the steam locomo-
tive in the very year of the Rainhill trials—and more than a decade
before the Victorian railway mania. More interesting is the reference
to Sussex and Huntingdonshire—both notorious poverty black
spots of the period—as the survival of their seventeenth-century and
mediaeval architecture into the twentieth century shows. Sussex in
particular, but also to a lesser degree Huntingdonshire, had by 1930,
with the coming of the railways, become prosperous commuter
belts, while the West Riding of Yorkshire was already plunging
towards Orwellian depression. The 'machines constructed on principles yet undiscovered', with its convenient clichéd vagueness, is
also a shot well ahead of its time. Such forecasts were common
enough by the 1880s when the young H.G. Wells was attending the
Normal School of Science in South Kensington, but in 1830 a leap of
imagination beyond steam was rare. Which brings us, of course, to
the one failure in Macaulay's list—a prophecy as notable for its
inaccuracy as the others were accurate—the notion that 'cultivation,
rich as a flower-garden, will be carried up to the very tops of Ben
Nevis and Helvellyn.'

To be fair, it is in one sense the victim of the other forecasts'
success. As Macaulay makes clear, he is *not*, in reality, indulging in
the kind of futurology later to be practised by Jules Verne, Wells, and
Kipling with such prescience. He is looking for a stick to beat
Southey with, and his weapon is projection of past trends.

[3] *Literary Essays*, p. 133.

We prophesy nothing; but this we say: If any person had told the Parliament which met in perplexity and terror after the crash of 1720 that in 1830 the wealth of England would surpass all their wildest dreams, that the annual revenue would equal the principal of that debt which they considered as an intolerable burden, that for one man of ten thousand pounds then living there would be five men of fifty thousand pounds, that London would be twice as large and twice as populous, and that nevertheless the rate of mortality would have diminished to one half of what it then was ... that stage-coaches would run from London to York in twenty-four hours, that men would be in the habit of sailing without wind, and would be beginning to ride without horses, our ancestors would have given as much credit to the prediction as they gave to Gulliver's Travels.[4]

He is writing not as a prophet, but as a *historian*: looking forwards to illuminate the past. Population increases, revolutions in transport, rising standards of living, more home comforts; these are the bread-and-butter of a Whig historian—their very familarity makes us blind to them, he implies, unless we illustrate what is happening by a leap into the future. Where such a method fails, of course, is in predicting revolutions of sensibility: in this case, a totally new attitude towards landscape in general, and towards the wilderness in particular. Nothing in the National Debt of the Hanoverians or Charles II could have pointed Macaulay towards the foundation of the National Trust and the Lake District National Park.

Macaulay's idea of landscape, and the consummation of its improvement as flower gardens (or their equivalents) on the peaks of the Scottish Highlands and the Lake District declares its ancestry as unmistakably as his views of economic progress. Indeed, it is a part of his economic beliefs, and, like them, it is in some ways a deeply conservative vision—or rather, combination of visions, for we can detect in his throwaway prophecy elements of two quite distinct landscape traditions. The first is the eighteenth-century habit of identifying beauty with usefulness. An aesthetically pleasing landscape is a well-cultivated landscape. Where man is not clearly in evidence, Nature is barren. Though it is by no means their only attitude towards landscape, it is one found frequently in Arthur Young[5] and in Cobbett—we see it, for instance, very clearly in

[4] *Literary Essays*, p. 133.
[5] Arthur Young, *Tours in England and Wales* (London School of Economics Reprint No 14, 1932), pp. 6–7.

Cobbett's reply to Young's enthusiasm for the richness of the Vale of
Farnham, when he points out that his native town is 'a mere little
strip' bounded north or south by 'barrenness' and a 'sterling sterility'
of sand 'upon which a blade of grass will no more grow than it would
upon the iron plate of this American stove by which I am now
writing . . .'[6] In particular, the idea of cultivating a hill or mountain
right to its summit had a particular fascination as a symbol of man's
conquest and domination of nature. W.T. Pomeroy, author of *A
General View of the Agriculture of Worcestershire* (1794) displays this
fascination in all its complexity:

> If the Aberley and Whitley hills occasion some irregularity to the
> frame, they will scarcely be thought to take off from the beauty of
> the piece; these, and the adjoining hills, rising with a bold front,
> and most of them cultivated to their summits, recall to the mind
> the enthusiastic description of Italy; and the sheep, hanging as it
> were, from the brows of others, illustrate the much admired idea
> of the Roman bard.[7]

I agree with John Barrell that it is not easy to disentangle the various
aesthetic attitudes revealed in this passage. But what concerns us
here is not so much how the Claudian frame of reference is employed, as the imagery of that last sentence. At first glance it appears
to be similar to that of Dyer's *Grongar Hill* in its use of metaphors
derived from the human body to delineate the landscape; a closer
inspection, however, suggests that the 'brows' of the hills, rising
'with a bold front' are not so much anthropomorphic as *architectural*.
Grongar Hill is actually 'crowned' by a ruined castle; here the castle
is, as it were, *itself* metaphorical. It is the agriculture, either arable or
pastoral, that is seen as an act of conquest of the otherwise disorderly
and threatening landscape. The obligatory tower or ruin in a Claude
or sometimes in an early Turner covertly implied man's domination
of the wilderness—or, as in *Grongar Hill* itself, the reverse: a symbol
of man's vanity and pride, with ravens, foxes, and toads re-
establishing themselves where man had thought to triumph. The
carrying of agriculture to the summit of some wild peak is thus an act
of occupation of potentially hostile territory in a tradition of military
imagery. Macaulay seems to echo Pomeroy's very phraseology.

[6] *Cobbett's Tour in Scotland and the Northern Counties of England in 1832*
(London, 1833), p. 260.
[7] pp. 7–8; cited by John Barrell, *The Idea of Landscape and the Sense of Place,
1730–1840* (Cambridge, 1972), p. 76.

This is not a tradition that is necessarily anti-conservationist, but it is conservation on man's terms. Cobbett writes with evident delight of the custom in one part of Hertfordshire:

> ... to leave a *border* round the ploughed part of the fields to bear grass and to make hay from, so that, the grass being now made into hay, every cornfield has a closely mowed grass walk about ten feet wide all round it, between the corn and the hedge. This is most beautiful! The hedges are now full of the shepherd's rose, honeysuckles, and all sorts of wild flowers; so that you are upon a grass walk, with this most beautiful of all flower gardens and shrubberies on your one hand, and with the corn on the other. And thus you go from field to field (on foot or on horseback), the sort of corn, the sort of underwood and timber, the shape and size of the fields, the height of the hedge-rows, the height of the trees, all continually varying. Talk of *pleasure-grounds* indeed! What, that man ever invented, under the name of pleasure-grounds, can equal these fields in Hertfordshire?[8]

The comparison with pleasure-gardens makes it clear how far Cobbett's desire for preservation of wild flowers and wildlife is within a context of domesticity.

This is, of course, the second strand in Macaulay. His cultivation is not merely expressing utility but lushness. As those who have climbed them will recall, Ben Nevis and Helvellyn are, on their upper slopes, as fine a pair of natural slag-heaps as one may find anywhere. Southey himself, on his tour of Scotland, in 1819, had described Ben Nevis as 'a precipitous, rugged, stony, uninviting mountain, looking as if it had been riven from the summit to the base, and half of it torn away. It is an aweful mass ...'[9] In his *Colloquies*, moreover, among other forms of public works to alleviate unemployment, he had suggested the reclamation of waste and unprofitable land. Macaulay, therefore, though he had not read Southey's opinion of Ben Nevis, is actually responding to what he *had* read of Southey's suggestions for land improvement. *Laissez-faire* will make Ben Nevis bloom. Certainly the idea of cultivation 'rich as a flower-garden' is outrageous hyperbole, but that is perhaps a useful reminder that this is the tone of the whole passage. To assert

[8] *Rural Rides*, eds. G.D.H. and M. Cole (London, 1930), I.80; cited by James Sambrook, *William Cobbett* (London, 1973), p. 193.
[9] *Journal of a Tour in Scotland 1819* (Edinburgh, 1972), p. 202.

as wealthy a future for Sussex or Huntingdonshire as for the West Riding of Yorkshire would have seemed no less hyperbolic to many sceptical contemporaries. The idea of landscape-as-garden has a long history and it has been well-documented. The biblical story of Eden, the Earthly Paradise of Dante, mediaeval and renaissance allegories have all contributed to the rich deposit of association that Macaulay is able to invoke by that simple adjectival clause. Here the stress is not on utility, but on sanctuary, moral order, and harmony; not the Burkeian sublime, but the 'beautiful'.

And here, of course, is where Macaulay's rhetorical synthesis encounters trouble. The point that he wishes to make against Southey's argument is, at bottom, an economic one. *Laissez-faire* is for him the most efficient and productive way of encouraging agriculture as it is of any other economic enterprise. 'We firmly believe that five hundred thousand pounds subscribed by individuals for railroads or canals would produce more advantage to the public than five millions voted by Parliament for the same purpose.'[10] But the argument cannot be allowed to develop into one of 'utility' versus 'beauty' as it had already done in town-planning and architecture: Pugin's *Contrasts* is only three years away. In landscape utility *is* beauty. A landscape conquered to the highest peaks by agriculture is thus a visible aesthetic expression of progress. The agrarian improvements begun in the middle of the previous century will, Macaulay implies, continue to a point we cannot yet imagine. The same spirit that greened the sandy waste of the Norfolk Brecklands will make a cottage garden out of Ben Nevis or Helvellyn. Yet, ironically, this hyperbolic faith in the future of scientific farming misses the conclusion of its own economic logic. If there are really to be such dramatic improvements in agricultural method, then it would not be necessary to farm Helvellyn anyway. The rich soils of the midlands and East Anglia would suffice to feed the swelling population of fifty millions, and so far from prospering, agriculture on the hill farms would become more and more marginal. And so it was to prove: as A.G. Street's accounts of Welsh hill farming in the 1930s illustrate clearly.[11] The only conceivable reason for farming Helvellyn would be as a defiant demonstration that it *could* be done—as an assertion of man's mastery over the most inhospitable and bleak places of the land. But the purpose *then* would be un-

[10] *Literary Essays*, pp. 111–12.
[11] *Farmer's Glory* (London, 1932).

equivocally aesthetic—an attempt to beautify a place of no inherent agricultural value: precisely the kind of misuse and waste of resources Macaulay has attributed to public funding. Macaulay's landscape synthesis deconstructs itself.

But even rhetorical hyperboles have their meaning. Why, for instance, Helvellyn? Why not the Scafells, higher mountains in the Lake District and even worse slag-heaps, or Skiddaw, nearly as high and towering directly above Keswick where Southey actually lived? Could it be that Helvellyn had other, particular, associations for Macaulay? Though not far from Southey, it was closer to Rydal Mount and the man who, more than any other, was to ensure that nobody, on either aesthetic or economic pretext, was to try any agricultural experiments on Helvellyn's summit—the effectual patron of the conservation lobby—William Wordsworth.

The story of Wordsworth's influence on the landscape of the Lake District is almost as complex as the story of its influence on him. But for our purposes the crudest of outlines will suffice. By the mid-years of the century Wordsworth's own crusade to defend the landscape against 'utility' had gained two powerful groups of allies. One was centred on Ruskin and his circle at Brantwood on Coniston, the other on the Arnolds just across the valley from Rydal Mount at Fox How. The youthful Matthew Arnold was taken to visit the Great Man. His niece, though she did not have quite the proper credentials of birth in the valley, made up for it by returning from Tasmania at the age of two, and (later) making the Lake District setting a vital part of two of her best-selling novels. Mrs Humphry Ward's *Robert Elsmere* and *Helbeck of Banisdale* both use an unmistakably biblical typology in relation to the local typography. When Catherine, in *Robert Elsmere*, wishes to leave the mundane world and walk apart in peace of spirit, she does so not by retreating into a garden, as a former generation might have done, but by ascending into the awful sublimity of the mountains above Long Whindale—the Helvellyn range. Though no friend of Arnoldian theology, the vicar of Wray at this time (the closing years of the century) was Canon Rawnsley, an avid Wordsworthian. It was he who, together with Octavia Hill (from the Ruskin circle) and Sir Robert Hunter, a lawyer, founded the National Trust in 1895 for the express purpose of preventing the desecration of areas of outstanding natural beauty by property developers or inappropriate farming methods.[12] He was also soon to

[12] See W.T. Hill, *Octavia Hill: Pioneer of the National Trust* (London, 1956).

be aided by the not inconsiderable funds supplied by another
Wordsworthian, a shy young woman from London whom he had
befriended as a child. It was Rawnsley who had advised Beatrix
Potter on the publication of *Peter Rabbit*, and the income from the
phenomenal sales of her books went first to buy Hill Top Farm at
Sawrey in the Furness fells, and then over four thousand acres of
threatened Lake District territory which were presented to the Trust
at her death. She was also the means of rescuing an extraordinary
little notebook which had turned up in her ice-house at Hill Top:
Ann Tyson's Prompt Book.[13] Ann Tyson is immortalized as the
'dame' with whom the schoolboy Wordsworth had lodged in the
1780s when he was attending Hawkshead Grammar School. From it
we know in almost indecent detail his day-to-day life: his diet, his
debts, who else was lodging in the house (as it happens, two other
budding poets) and much else besides. It seems a fitting piece of
serendipity that this unique record of the poet's childhood should
have come to light in the property of the person who had done more
than any other to preserve the landscape he knew unravaged by
Macaulayan progress.

   It would probably not have seemed so to Wordsworth. He was,
by the latter part of his life, deeply distressed by the newly fashion-
able custom of painting the stone cottages white. He was also worried by the rapid spread of bracken across the fells, which gave them
their now characteristic reddish-brown appearance in autumn and
winter. But both white cottages and encroaching braken were
nothing to the threat posed in 1844 by the Kendal to Windermere
Railway:

> Is then no nook of English ground secure
> From rash assault? Scheme of retirement sown
> In youth, and mid the busy world kept pure
> As when their earliest flowers of hope were blown,
> Must perish;—how can they this blight endure?
> And must he too the ruthless change bemoan
> Who scorns a false utilitarian lure
> Mid his paternal fields at random thrown?
> Baffle the threat, bright Scene, from Orrest-head
> Given to the pausing traveller's rapturous glance:
> Plead for thy peace, thou beautiful romance
> Of nature; and, if human hearts be dead,
> Speak, passing winds; ye torrents, with your strong
> And constant voice, protect against the wrong.

[13] See T.W. Thompson, *Wordsworth's Hawkshead* (Oxford, 1970).

Wordsworth's argument here provides an interesting commentary on Macaulay's. In the opening lines the military metaphor implicit in the older tradition is now deliberately reversed. 'English ground' is under threat from the 'assault' of progress. 'Nook' is rather a special word in Wordsworth's vocabulary. It occurs twice, for instance, at key points in *Nutting*—both times in a sexually charged context:

> Among the woods,
> And o'er the pathless rocks, I forc'd my way
> Until, at length, I came to one dear nook
> Unvisited, where not a broken bough
> Droop'd with its wither'd leaves, ungracious sign
> Of devastation, but the hazels rose
> Tall and erect, with milk-white clusters hung,
> A virgin scene!   (ll. 13–20)

The violation of this 'virgin scene' by Wordsworth himself is even more explicit:

> Then up I rose,
> And dragg'd to earth both branch and bough, with crash
> And merciless ravage; and the shady nook
> Of hazels, and the green and mossy bower
> Deform'd and sullied, patiently gave up
> Their quiet being . . .   (ll. 42–7)

Intrusion and despoliation of this nook is an act of rape. The 'rash assault' of the railway is, it seems, more than a mere military metaphor. The conquest and possession of the land by the forces of industrial progress is not fruitful and productive, but a barren assertion of will: a sexual assault. The interweaving of garden and vaginal imagery is centuries old: a 'nook' is for Wordsworth what a garden signified in an earlier vocabulary. The *hortus conclusus* is a place of stimulation and refinement of the senses. Comparisons between *Nutting* and Marvell's *Garden*, for instance, make the point clearly.

> Fair Quiet, have I found thee here,
> And Innocence, thy sister dear?
> Mistaken long, I sought you then
> In busy companies of men.
> Your sacred plants, if here below,
> Only among the plants will grow;
> Society is all but rude
> To this delicious solitude.

No white nor red was ever seen
So amorous as this lovely green . . .   (ll. 9–18)

The nook is the place of retirement and seclusion where
Wordsworth sat 'voluptuous . . . among the flowers, and the flowers
. . . play'd'—a place simultaneously of lush sensuousness and
innocence until the entry of man. Wordsworth is here drawing upon
the same gardening imagery as Macaulay, but whereas, of course,
Macaulay wanted to make the garden into a macrocosm,
universalize it, and spread it across the landscape, Wordsworth
retains the sense that a 'garden', even if it is natural rather than
artificial, is a microcosm. A nook that embraces the whole of
England is not a nook. Macaulay had, as it were, violated nature by
confusing microcosm with macrocosm; the beautiful with the
sublime. It is that Burkeian antithesis that lies behind Wordsworth's
sestet invoking the 'bright Scene, from Orrest-head' and in the final
couplet, the landscape of the sublime, 'the winds and torrents' to
protest against the rape of the beautiful. Each requires its opposite.
What Wordsworth is defending is not just a landscape but an *order* in
an almost mediaeval sense.

In Wordsworth's disciple, Ruskin, this sense of rape of an
established metaphysical order is seen specifically in terms of the
re-born Greek classicism of the Victorians. Protesting against the
construction of another railway—this time through Monsal Dale in
Derbyshire—he wrote:

> There was a rocky valley between Buxton and Bakewell, once
> upon a time, divine as the vale of Tempe; you might have seen
> gods there morning and evening—Apollo and all the sweet
> Muses of Light, walking in fair procession on the lawns of it . . .
> You cared neither for gods nor grass, but for cash . . . You
> enterprised a railroad through the valley . . . The valley is gone,
> and the gods with it; and now, every fool in Buxton can be at
> Bakewell in half-an-hour, and every fool in Bakewell at
> Buxton.[14]

This suspicion of the need to travel or sightsee by 'every fool in
Buxton' (or, as it may be, Kendal) is one fully shared by

---

[14] *Fors Clavigera* Letter 5 (quoted again in the final chapter of *Praeterita*).
Cited by Richard Jenkyns, *The Victorians and Ancient Greece* (Oxford, 1980),
pp. 181–2.

Wordsworth. In a letter to *The Morning Post* accompanying his
sonnet, he explains his feelings of outrage more clearly. The appeal
to the order and harmony of innocence coexists with something so
unexpected that it is easy to miss the full force of what he is saying. It
is true that he is alarmed by the thought of hordes of trippers pouring
into the Lake District—he does not object to 'tourists' because the
very word precludes the notion of a railway'[15]—because he feels that

> the perception of what has acquired the name of picturesque and
> romantic scenery is so far from being intuitive, that it can be
> produced only by a slow and gradual process of culture, and . . . as
> a consequence . . . the humbler ranks of society are not, and
> cannot be, in a state to gain material benefits from a more speedy
> access than they have now to this beautiful region.[16]

Understanding landscape is a slow process of growth and education.
The old Wordsworth is a little worried that publicizing such a view
might look as if he is going back on his youthful commitment to the
cause of the poor, but he stuck to his position in spite of a storm of
abuse. What he does not say in so many words, but is always
evident, is that his admiration was always for the rural poor, and in
particular for the Cumberland 'statesmen' or smallholders, not for
the urban masses—for whom he had expressed some contempt in
The Excursion. Now, however, in this sonnet he strikes a new note.
The 'schemes of retirement' sound at first as if they belong to the
same world as the 'garden' imagery, but the word had acquired its
more modern meaning well before Wordsworth's time, and the
contrast of youth and age underlines its main sense. This is not so
much the contemplative aesthetic withdrawal of a Marvell or a
William Iden, but a home for old age: perhaps not for too many of
the Manchester bourgeoisie, but certainly for the Arnolds, Ruskin,
and other members of the educated classes capable of appreciating
the landscape. Wordsworth's letter to the *Morning Post* is an
astonishingly academic piece, stressing what a *new* phenomenon was
the appreciation of mountain scenery. He cites passages from
Evelyn, Ray, Bishop Burnet, 'the other Burnet', and Gray, the poet,
all of whom reacted with horror to the sublimity and grandeur of the

---

[15] His point seems to be the semantic one that 'tourists' go on 'tours'—
that is, travel in circuits—whereas railways shuttle.

[16] 'Kendal and Windamere Railway', *The Prose Works of William Wordsworth*, eds. W.J.B. Owen and J.W. Smyser (Oxford, 1972), III.349.

high peaks and the loneliness. His point is that there is a revolution in sensibility in progress, and that the railway, with its offer of cheap and easy access to the wilderness, will destroy the very thing the more discerning travellers are in search of. It belongs, in effect, to the world of the old sensibility, not the new.

But Wordsworth is also playing politics in a manner worthy of Disraeli—as the fact that he chose to make his attack via a national paper, *The Morning Post*, indicates. Alongside the Lakeland 'statesman' whose rural patrimony is threatened by the 'false utilitarian lure' must stand those whose future plans for retirement will be blighted by the projected railway. This is a point he clarifies in his letter:

> Alongside the ancient inheritances of the yeomen, surely worthy of high respect, are interspersed through the entire district villas, most of them with such small domains attached that the occupants would be hardly less annoyed by a railway passing through their neighbour's ground than through their own.[17]

What Wordsworth is trying to do is to put together a political coalition of local interests and visitors with an equal stake in preserving the landscape as it is—in short, Michael must put aside his suspicion of the wicked city and make common cause with the Arnolds, Ruskins, Rawnsleys, and Beatrix Potter.

The corollary of this argument is even more interesting if we turn back to Macaulay's original prophecies. The population of fifty millions, better fed, clad, and housed than in the early nineteenth century, travelling by railway (or even, let us suppose, by machines constructed on principles yet undiscovered) will fight to *preserve* the very distinction between the garden and the wilderness that Macaulay assumed would be obliterated by progress because that distinction is an essential element in the natural harmony between man and the environment. Burke's distinction, we recall, is primarily a psychological one, and it is precisely that psychological correspondence that Wordsworth focuses on in the Preface to *The Excursion*. There is no contradiction here: as Wordsworth saw, the preservation of the wilderness is a direct human consequence of population pressure and increased prosperity. If we needed an example of this we need look no further than Beatrix Potter herself,

[17] *Prose Works*, III.352.

whose family money came from investments in the railways, and whose passionate interest in natural history and rural life was encouraged by a city upbringing and an emotionally undernourished home-life. Of such stuff are Wordsworthians made.

Yet, Wordsworth, too, for all his perspicacity, had also failed to see some of the consequences of his argument. As we have seen, Macaulay, invoking the name of progress, had in fact conceived the question of landscape in essentially conservative and outmoded terms that eventually contradicted themselves; Wordsworth, apparently the conservative, is correct in seeing himself as the spearhead of a radical shift in aesthetic sensibility that will, in the end, mean a quite new attitude to the wilderness. What he could not adequately come to terms with was the fact that change in the present is no different from change in the past. The landscape of the wilderness is as much in a process of change as the landscape of the garden. In his second sonnet on the Kendal and Windermere Railway he concentrates specifically on the changes to the landscape made by man.

> Proud were ye, Mountains, when, in times of old,
> Your patriot sons, to stem invasive war,
> Intrenched your brows; ye gloried in each scar:
> Now, for your shame, a Power, the Thirst of Gold,
> That rules o'er Britain like a baneful star,
> Wills that your peace, your beauty, shall be sold,
> And clear way made for her triumphal car
> Through the beloved retreats your arms enfold!
> Heard YE that Whistle? As her long-linked Train
> Swept onwards, did the vision cross your view?
> Yes, ye were startled;—and, in balance true,
> Weighing the mischief with the promised gain,
> Mountains, and Vales, and Floods, I call on you
> To share the passion of a just disdain.

The complex chain of imagery we have been following throughout this paper persists with astonishing consistency. We are dealing with an anthropomorphized landscape of war. The proud mountains, like old warriors, bear scars upon their brows. But this time the war is not metaphorical but real and human: the scars are iron-age hill forts. These scars of the past, however, have healed, and like the ruins in a Claude landscape or on Grongar Hill, are a moral enhancement to the scenery rather than a disfigurement of it. The difference between the ancient earthworks and the modern railway embankments and cuttings, Wordsworth argues, is primarily one of *motive* rather than aesthetics. The one is a symbol of honourable patriotism, the other of naked greed. The argument, like the quality of the verse, is distinctly doubtful. The invocation of the ancient Britons, like that of the Saxon liberties by Macaulay and other Whigs, though a matter of intense and real emotion for many at this period,[18] was never much more than a rhetorical gesture. Moreover, the landscape is made up of earthworks, not motive. Like Macaulay, Wordsworth is weakest on the economics—failing to see that prosperity would do more than poverty to preserve his wilderness of mountains and vales and floods. Nor could he recognize that the earthworks of the railway would, in their turn, be assimilated into the ever-changing synthesis of the rural landscape, and evoke, at any rate for some in the twentieth century, the same aesthetic feelings as whitewashed cottages and bracken-covered fells. When the railway line from Kendal to Windermere was closed recently there was a public outcry, not least from conservationists. It has now been re-opened, linked with the high-speed passenger trains from London to Scotland, to offer day-return trips from Euston to Windermere with a five-hour stay in the Lakes.

Two other steam railways, one on the far side of Windermere, the other in Eskdale, operate purely for the tourist trade and are considered an enhancement of the environment. The National Trust approves.

[18] For the emotive significance of these images see John Burrow, *A Liberal Descent: Victorian Historians and the English Past* (Cambridge, 1982).

Notes on collector and contributors

G.A. Wilkes is Challis Professor of English Literature at the University of Sydney. He has edited *The Remains* of Fulke Greville, Lord Brooke (1965) and the *Complete Plays* of Ben Jonson (1981–2), and is general editor of the Challis Shakespeare. He is also the author of *The Stockyard and the Croquet Lawn: Literary Evidence for Australian Cultural Development* (1981) and of *A Dictionary of Australian Colloquialisms* (1978, 1985). He has been editor of *Southerly*, the journal of the Sydney Branch of the English Association, since 1963.

James Simpson was educated at the Universities of Melbourne and Oxford; since 1981 he has been a lecturer in English at Westfield College, University of London. He has articles on *Piers Plowman* forthcoming in *RES, MAE, Neuphilologische Mitteilungen, Notes and Queries*, and in a *festschrift* for G.H. Russell, which he is co-editing.

David Frost has been Professor of English in the University of Newcastle, New South Wales, since 1977, and is currently Head of Department. Previously, he was Fellow and Director of Studies in English at St John's College, Cambridge, and University Assistant Lecturer in English. His publications include *The School of Shakespeare: the Influence of Shakespeare on English Drama, 1600–42*, an edition of the *Selected Plays of Thomas Middleton*, a translation, *The Psalms: a New Translation for Worship*, and articles on Shakespeare, on religious language, and on literary translation. He has served on the Liturgical Commissions of the Anglican Church in England and Australia, and was one of the compilers of *The Alternative Service Book, 1980*.

Ian Donaldson is Professor of English and Director of the Humanities Research Centre at the Australian National University, Canberra. His books include *The World Upside-Down: Comedy From Jonson to Fielding*, *The Rapes of Lucretia: A Myth and its Transformations*, and editions of *Ben Jonson Poems* for the Oxford Standard Authors and of *Ben Jonson* for the new Oxford Authors series.

John Hardy is Professor of English at the Australian National University and Secretary of the Australian Academy of the Humanities. Besides editions of Johnson's *Rasselas* and *Lives of the Poets*, his books include *Reinterpretations: Essays on Poems by Milton, Pope and Johnson, Samuel Johnson: A Critical Study*, and *Jane Austen's Heroines: Intimacy in Human Relationships*.

After many years in the English Department of the University of Sydney, John Burrows was appointed Professor of English at the University of Newcastle, New South Wales, in 1976. He held the Commonwealth Fellowship of St John's College, Cambridge, in 1979–80. Apart from *Jane Austen's 'Emma'* (Sydney, 1968), his published work lies in articles treating a wide range of literary topics but concentrating, at one time, on Patrick White and more recently on Jane Austen. Since 1979 he has been engaged with the matters treated in the present paper. He is continuing to work in new directions of this kind, focusing especially on the evidence of letter-writing as a possible bridge between literary and 'natural' language.

Andrew Lincoln teaches in the English Department, Westfield College, University of London. His main academic interests are Romantic poetry and twentieth-century literature. He has published articles on Blake in *Blake: an Illustrated Quarterly* and in *Bulletin of Research in the Humanities*.

Stephen Prickett has been Professor of English at the Australian National University in Canberra since 1983. He was previously Chairman of English at the University of Sussex. His published books include *Coleridge and Wordsworth: The Poetry of Growth* (1970), *Romanticism and Religion* (1976), and *Victorian Fantasy* (1979). A new book, *Words and the 'Word': Language, Poetics, and Biblical Interpretation* is due out from Cambridge University Press in 1986.